5th Dimensional

Consciousness

2nd Edition

Profound Ways to Awaken Your Potential and Align with Future

Contact

By Joanna L. Ross

5th Dimensional Consciousness: Profound Ways to Awaken Your Potential and Align with Future Contact, 2nd Edition

by Joanna L. Ross

Published 2016 by Universal Unity

Calgary, Alberta

http://universalunity.ca

Copyright © Joanna L. Ross

Layout and editing by Linda Bolton-Holder

Printed in the United States

First edition published by The Light Network: 2015

ISBN-13: 978-1537605043

ISBN-10: 1537605046

Endorsements

In 5th Dimensional Consciousness—5 Profound Ways to Raise Your Vibrational Frequency—A Path to Universal Unity author Joanna L. Ross takes us to the next step of human evolution and experience as she discusses this topic that is so near and dear to her own heart. Joanna's insights are based on research, on channelled materials, and on her own direct experience. They are presented in an exciting way as she extends to you; her reader, her deep understanding and profound wisdom regarding a whole array of topics, such as planetary ascension, the energetic planetary shift we are currently experiencing, first landings, and first contacts with inter-dimensional and extraterrestrial species, and how to awaken without fear. Joanna has taken a bold step with this book; anyone who reads it will be sure to reach for more.

I have known Joanna L. Ross professionally and personally for many years, and have watched her unfold as a seeker, a leader, a teacher, and I am overjoyed to see her progress to author and world-changer."

~Sandy Anastasi, Psychic Channel, intuitive astrologer, and soul coach

Are you ready to awaken to your highest potential? As human beings comprised of light energy, it's time to connect with our higher self and align our mind, body, and spirit with the global consciousness as we prepare for new experiences on a planetary level.

In her book, 5th Dimensional Consciousness—5 Profound Ways to Raise Your Vibrational Frequency—A Path to Universal Unity, author and teacher Joanna L. Ross shares her personal journey of awakening along with the path of evolution for humanity and the evolution of Gaia herself. Joanna's book takes you on her journey of self-exploration, introspection, awakening, and profound awareness and communication with the universe.

Ask yourself, what synchronicity has led me to this book, then open, and allow yourself to explore the greater mysteries.

~Kala Ambrose, award-winning author, wisdom teacher and host of the *Explore Your Spirit with Kala Show*

5th Dimensional Consciousness by Joanna L. Ross is a must read for the spiritual traveler and anyone seeking true insight into the collective consciousness. With great insight, research, and personal experience, Joanna inspires the reader to seek a higher vibrational frequency and access a deeper level of awareness by skillfully demonstrating her own. I loved reading this book but even more importantly, I loved the way I felt after I did.

~Marguerite Manning, Llewellyn, worldwide bestselling author of *Cosmic Karma, Understanding Your Contract with the Universe*

We are multi-dimensional aspects of All That Is. Like the specks of star dust that light the cosmos, we all contain the vibration and essence of Source. In various genetic forms, colours, physical dispositions, and vibrational frequencies, we all mirror back to the Creator our unique expression and creative potential. Diverse, Divine, and infinitely profound, this is the journey of Gaia and her people as we experience the profundity of Creation and as we ascend into a new vibrational bedding within the sky.

We are pieces of this glorious Universal puzzle, all valued, all valid, all required. And so the journey has begun. In oneness, in love and light, we stand."

~Joanna L. Ross

Acknowledgements

The process of ascension allows us to not only expand our understanding and link with All That Is, but also to remember our link and entanglement with all others within the Universe we experience. This process opens our potential to greater and expanded experiences that enliven our consciousness to heightened states. It is in these heightened states that we fully remember our Divine encoding; the essence from which we came bursting to this experience with hope, reverence, and the promise of an awakening that would reverberate throughout Creation. This experience would not have been the journey it has been, without the help of these Divine souls:

Eric R. Perez ~ for your continued positivity and support of all my dreams.

Joshua, Hannah, Zachary ~ for your infinite energy that inspires me, empowers me, and enlightens me in ways that only children can. I will always seek answers to expand upon your insatiable curiosity, and gifted light. Your souls have changed me, THANK YOU.

Chris Mariotti ~ for taking all of my concepts and ideas, and creating the portal that inspires so many around the world. You are amazing. THANK YOU!

Keidi Keating ~ for taking the plethora of written works and creating another dream so that all can enjoy and expand. This would not have been possible without the many hours you have contributed. Deepest gratitude!

Wendy Kennedy and the P's! ~ for your unconditional support and guidance as I navigate the energetic shifting and exploration through uncharted territory. I have gained immeasurable confidence from your teachings and I would not be able to put my experiences into words if it had not been for your loving encouragement to embrace my Divine essence. Deepest gratitude for your validations and expertise.

Sandy Anastasi ~ a colleague, a friend, and my first spiritual teacher. Thank you for your constant encouragement, inspiration, and commitment to bringing awareness and light to our planet.

Kala Ambrose ~ a colleague, friend, and one of the most amazing women in this incredible arena. You are a maverick and leader for the light you inspire. Thank you for cheering me on as my path has unfolded.

My Earth Family ~ deepest gratitude to my parents, Ken

and MariLynn, for their Divine timing and creating the life in which I exist. You have offered the most profound life lessons and a work ethic. Your integrity has always inspired me to reach for the stars, and for that, I am eternally grateful. To my beautiful sisters, Gina and Tania, for giving me the opportunity to learn, gain wisdom, and grow just as you have. You are pure within your hearts, and I am grateful to have you in my life. Never stop seeking the answers you crave, for your light is so profound and others will be blessed by it. Thank you!

And of course, the best for last - my newly awakened gratitude to Creation, God, Source, and All That Is, for the impeccable design and benevolence in all that You do. Without the loving lifeline that You have sent to assist me, I would not be here today. With the all the magic, light, deepest gratitude, and love I am able to offer, THANK YOU.

Celestial Gratitude

I am in the deepest state of gratitude in every hour of every day for the myriad of beings, my celestial family, friends, councils that I work with in other realms, for their unconditional support, energetic work, and guidance and ever-lighted presence with my excitement and passion.

I offer my appreciation to my spirit guides, the angelic realm, elementals, and my Higher Self that continually envelopes me in love and guidance, and forever offers me the synchronistic opportunities to further my growth and offerings to humanity. Thank you for continually steering me gently to the path that I was destined to be on, particularly all the times that I strayed.

To all beings that seek the light within, may we all walk united and step forward in love.

Dedication

This book is a gift from my Higher Self to you. It is the result of years of dedication to the ascension process, global enlightenment, and a passion for Universal knowledge.

I dedicate this book to my three gorgeous, intuitive children, Joshua, Hannah, and Zachary. I learn from them every day and these lessons have proven to be the most valuable insight into understanding the fine balance between Earthly experience and what unfolds as one expands. They bring the element of heaven to Earth.

I would also like to thank with my extensive Universal family for the unique and loving experiences that have inspired me beyond all Earthly words. Your instruction has allowed me to create the experiences and gain the insights that guide me on this path to ascension.

I express my deepest gratitude to you all the Pleiadians, the many beings from Sirius, Tecarians, Alpha Centauri, the energetic family from Arcturus, Cassiopeia, Orion, and the myriad of other watchful and dedication beings of Light, who serve in commitment and love for all of humanity. The constant and benevolent energetic work you inject into every aspect of my life, and your guidance, love, and wisdom has brought me from fearful, worried, and disconnected, to an awakened and engaged spirit essence with dedication to expand and learn in as many ways that you have taught. Thank you for your service, love, wisdom, and light.

Table of Contents

Preface

The scope of the writings herein, I offer with the greatest excitement and passion for the potential that humanity has to move beyond limitation in very profound ways. Through my own personal experiences, ascension study, and years of metaphysical and esoteric research, I have moved through various stages of enlightenment and awareness that can serve as somewhat of an Ascension Playbook, for those who desire to tap into multi-dimensional, ascension, and esoteric topics that heed the call of our profound spirit within.

I will walk the reader through various key aspects of the process of our ever-changing planetary environment, the physical changes, and symptoms that follow with a planetary shift, and how to maximize and enhance ascension activation, multi-dimensional communication, and really propel the entanglement and intimacy with Creation, Source, and all life that we are embodied with. Many great shifts have occurred since Gaia set on her path to ascend. And through every subtle and profound shift, there are still so many who move through life in a disconnected slumber; unaware of what is truly going on. My hope in writing the knowledge I have learned, and the wisdom that I have gained, is that those who find themselves seeking the deeper answers to life's stirring questions, know that their ability to transform their life from ordinary to extraordinary is all entirely possible in this new realm that we are all co-creating.

The creating of a new vibrational realm appears to be the work of geniuses or celestial merlins -- which in many respects it is -- but there is also a creative genius within each of us and it is part of the tremendous process that Gaia began long ago. As we enter into the 5th dimensional frequency, we will have learned the many lessons and themes that can allow humanity the opportunity to truly test what we are made of and fall in line with the masters, as we were always meant to. We will allow the fears, doubts, limitations, and chains of darkness fall away into the storybooks of our old version of who we use to be, and step up into the new illuminated galactic human of the now moment in Creation.

The path of ascension offers many things to humanity, but one gift that is unparalleled is that we understand for the first time in Earth's history that we are far from stuck, limited, or average. Regardless of what swirls around us in the media or what has been taught in our schools or social structures, we have altered the portal of potential just enough, to reveal the magical evidence of our innate power and know that we are true masters in Creation, just as any advanced celestial being may be. With every new powerful thought, powerful intention, and kind and loving act we are literally changing the face of Gaia. The resonance of this immense frequency cannot be denied, and our creative abilities give us access to the highest realm for anyone who is ready to step up into the shoes of the evolving human.

About eight years ago, while living a seemingly normal suburban life, I was beset by many personal challenges, but they propelled me onto this path of ascension. In one of my daily meditations, I connected for the first time with my profound spirit guides in what I call "my benevolent call to service." This experience was life altering when I was allowed to sense the invisible world of Universal energy. I have been truly hooked ever since that day more than eight years ago. I look back now and can see how even the most challenging of experiences were necessary for me to gain the level of understanding and awareness that I needed. For every turn, every choice, and every misguided action had to be taken for me to feel the sense of liberation I felt when the hand of Spirit showed me the potential of who I am. This level of profundity and spirit essence resides with every human being in Creation, and because I felt and learned what I did in that one experience, I made it my life's work to assist whomever allowed themselves to find their way to my offerings.

Every person on this planet has agreed to be here in this amazing time. Each person also carries within them a life theme, a higher purpose, or reason for choosing this Earthly experience. These greater life questions allow us to tap into the depths of our innate power and know that there are no accidents; it is no coincidence that you are here now. There is a Divine design to everything and if we understand our part in this reality game, if we are to understand the basics of Universal energy and our ability to tap into it to manifest anything we desire, then we will have the a magical life with angelic gifts and offerings at every turn. This is all entirely possible in the new Earth potential that we are now living in.

This path of awakening has brought me to a heightened level of knowingness and faith in our glorious Universe and the breathtaking and magical surprises that it holds. Profound knowingness is an attribute of ascension and one must dive deep within the darkest aspects of who we are to uncover the gem we all hold at the core of our being. These ascension and awakening experiences, will provide you with a profound sense of knowingness, and with that knowingness comes self-clarity. This, in itself my friends, is worth celebrating. When you experience the offered energetic synchronicities on your path to enlightenment, you will be magically aligned with many other higher resonating beings, energies, and elements and they all have your highest and best interest at heart, for your expansion is an expansion for the whole. These are just some of the energetic portals that will open to you when you commit to self-discovery.

We will live in harmony with Creation, with Gaia, and one another, for the process of ascension allows us to peek through the window of the inner self, reflect and realign so that our outer reality shifts with the love that is discovered within. Planetary ascension allows those who are ready to tap into the infinite potential to climb up for a taste of a new cosmic adventure as well as new and expanded personal discoveries.

This book will assist you in your process of evolution and in finding your true authentic self. With the myriad of spiritual coaching and soul-searching offerings that are now available, it can seem daunting to decide where to start. Just know that any inner reflective work that you do, regardless of what it is labelled, it is ascension work. The plethora of names, topics, paths, and terminology associated with ascension can make inner spiritual work feel like a wild chase. It really makes no difference what name you give for your inner work; just know that if this is your Divine timing to awaken and your soul will trigger you in any way it can to inspire change and expansion. You can be taken on an infinite number of paths, and be motivated in directions that you never would have dreamed, and all of this, is to answer the call of the soul and fulfil what has been written in your pre-life agreement.

We will unveil the various terms, phases, and symptoms of the incredible process called ascension and in this, offer peace of mind to those who just about to embark upon on their path of self-discovery. All of this inner work, the unveiling of your true authentic self, is really allowing the illumination of your spirit essence to be seen by Creation. We have agreed to be here, in these special times, so that we can offer our unique, creative expression on our path to remembrance. We all hold within us the keys to mastery and enlightenment. It is our birthright access all the infinite possibilities and experience the life that we truly desire. Mastery is not apportioned only to the special few. You create mastery the moment you align with our highest inner vibration, which will give you the inner glory of a greater entanglement with all of Creation. Shine and bring forth your inner light, for your offering will change the world and your perfect inner light will then be the inspiration that lights the way for others. Your authenticity is your unique creative expression and it is your key that can unlock the gifts, the treasures, and the experiences that bring you in alignment with your Divine soul blueprint.

As you gain confidence, insight, and a greater expanded point of view, the world and the reality you exist within, shifts and changes with you. Our reality is the mirror to what we allow ourselves to experience, and the greater awareness we have, the more profound our potential becomes. Our reality is not rigid, or immovable, it is pliable, malleable, and can offer whatever you desire to create. In your path of spiritual awakening, you will begin to experience the results of conscious creating, intentional living, and a heightened sense of awareness and all the beautiful offerings that it provides. In every moment, we have the potential to shift what we experience, and it is in these moment-for-moment lessons that we infinitely expand in a myriad of ways. Whether your desires are to create wealth, health, intimacy, wisdom, or a greater knowledge of your role and purpose upon this planet -- and within this cosmos -- any path of inner work and self-discovery is key to kick-start the magical unfolding that is you. This is why ascension work and spiritual mastery is an infinite path, and the soul will forever be the catalyst that propels us into seeking the answers it inherently craves.

Ascension not only allows for profound self-clarity, knowingness, and direction, but it ignites a deeper understanding for our existence from a grander point of view. We begin to relate all aspects of our life with profound inclusivity. Like putting the pieces to the puzzle together, piece by piece, we are all inter-connected and linked at a quantum level and it is what we call, Oneness. Our Universe, our world, and the potential of humanity, are attributes within the story of ascension and self-discovery, for we are all woven within it. We are remembering, dear lighted-ones, that we are divinely entangled, enmeshed, and interwoven with all of Creation. Nothing is left out of ascension and self-discovery and as we absorb and imbue such concepts of inclusivity, we drop the borders, boundaries, and judgements in order to allow us to co-create an illuminated new Earth that resonates and offers unlimited possibilities for everyone.

In asking the questions, "Why does life unfold as it does and how can I better tap into this experience to create what I truly desire and deserve?" you will ignite the spark that sets in motion Divine synchronicity. The further you seek, expand, and inquire, the further you move yourself toward the path that will elevate your experiences and refine your ever-changing personal frequency. All of these gifts, experiences, and self-discoveries are available to you, as they are your Divine legacy. Should you so desire to stake your claim for higher vibrational living or improved intimate connections with all life forms, then anything you desire to know, be, and experience will be offered to you. For every being within Creation has the same potential, yet most of humanity is simply unaware of it. The pages that follow will allow you to view ascension from a myriad of angles with guidance from one who has been studying and practicing these tips, hints, trials, and triumphs, and experienced a complete change in vibrational living. If I can move through what I did, then it is possible for others to create their own sense of brilliance and unlimited potential. It is also why I am so passionate about offering all that I have learned in my incredible unveiling.

There have been many gifts and secrets left unshared for far too long upon this planet and Gaia has waited a long time for humanity to tune into her pleas and rumblings. We have lived in a state of grave imbalance with nature and her callings, and now, with these powerful ascending energies, we are offered the opportunity to change everything we have ever known so that we can create peace, harmony, and balance to humanity. These writings are my own personal offerings and I do so with the purity of my heart to express what I know to be true about personal awakening, challenges, soul-purpose, multi-dimensional understanding and enhancement, new Earth, 5th dimensional living, our benevolent celestial teams, Source, re-igniting engagement, intimacy, passion, and ecstasy. All of this is the potential that humanity is finally remembering and it is the path of ascension.

What lies ahead, dear lighted-ones, in this moment of now that we are co-creating, is truly breathtaking and I am passionate about sharing all that I have learned, gained, and experienced on my profound journey. We are all about to embark upon a new mission, one that promises many surprises, triumphs, and many incredible discoveries for anyone who chooses to climb aboard. What lies ahead is the discovery of how utterly profound you truly are. In all that ascension may open to you, know your worthiness to create such brilliance, for when you tap into the unconditional love that resides within you, you will be forever changed. This is my unique expression and the gift that I offer, in gratitude and reverence for what ascension has given me.

~ Namaste

Introduction

As a collective consciousness, we have lived in a state of constant and relentless struggles between the ego aspect of who we are and the higher calling that begs to be expressed. Our true calling, our life purpose, our destined path is about to unfold with soulful whispers and synchronicity. For many lifetimes, we have been led astray with the limiting conditionings and social structures that have kept us in a state of spiritual laziness and intuitive slumber. In such states of limitation and unawareness, life literally passes by. Lifetime after lifetime, we gain insight and wisdom, but this lifetime -- this vibrational frequency -- is different, for we are being offered the opportunity to ascend into a 5th dimensional resonance.

To ascend, to move beyond limitation, fear, doubt, worry, judgement, and any other dark belief and emotion, we need to go within ourselves and reflect upon what we believe to be true about who we are, the world in which we live, and the nature of our potential. Until now, we often missed the grander lessons that would propel us on a path to enlightenment and we were stuck in similar limiting experiences and themes. As Gaia envelops us with profound ascension energies, potential, and support, we are offered a perfect state to lay the groundwork in order to experience a magical existence. Before now, our understanding of the heightened vibrational state of potential associated with ascension was limited to the transition time when we passed from mortality. This is no longer the case. In these amazing times of awakening, we have been given the opportunity to tap into these life-altering processes to ignite the latent talent and Divine spark that has been swimming within us from our very first incarnation.

In every incarnation, we have a set course of themes and lessons to enable us to achieve a greater state of knowing, or awareness than we had in previous lifetimes. Each lifetime brought us additional experiences, an expanded sense of self, and ultimately, a state of angelic bliss that we all envision will one day be offered. As crazy and far-fetched as this may sound, we no longer have to endure hundreds of lifetimes to achieve vibrational bliss because now we can create it in this lifetime right now and right here. Ascension energies and infinite celestial, angelic, and spiritual help are infusing every part of the globe. We now have a prime playing field in which any being can achieve the expanded state and heightened frequency of enlightenment. The question is, "How does one attain enlightenment, and what does planetary ascension mean to me, to Gaia, and the future of humanity?"

This book will show the many paths to understanding personal ascension, but first it is necessary to expand our understanding at a planetary level, and understand that all beings are perfectly designed by Source. The galaxy that Earth sits within, the Universe, the multi-verse, is all intimately involved with All That Is, and vice-verse, and if this is the case, then so too is Gaia. When we talk about ascension, we are talking about the alteration of energy at the quantum level, so every cell, molecule, and even smallest of aspect that we perceive to fit within the whole, is altered as we place focus upon it. As one small shift occurs, so too does the All, for all within existence is intimately connected.

In the many challenges and struggles that have occurred for humanity and for Gaia, there has been an overriding agenda to bring greater light, awareness, and potential to Gaia and to humanity. The Divine plan for planetary ascension is one of profound proportions. Many councils, celestial groups, and higher-realm beings have all been called upon to assist in the process of, what is now being called, the event of the cosmos. This unique event of planetary ascension does not occur overnight, and it will undoubtedly be taught throughout the Universe, for eons to come. As we collectively expand our 3rd dimensional resonance to a 5th dimensional state, we will captivate the attention of a myriad of beings, and the multi-verse will respond by elevating its vibration as well. Can you envision the immensity of this task, how an occupied planet can ascend from a slumbering 3rd dimensional frequency, and rise to that of a glowing 5th dimensional potential, and how much Divine benevolence and orchestration is involved at every stage of this extraordinary process? This is mind-boggling.

In benevolent desire to see humanity ascend beyond our current state, Gaia is offering a new dimensional frequency to help us transition. She offers a new potential for anyone who is ready to embark on this incredible mission. To accomplish such a profound planetary task, there is a great deal that needs to be done at every level. But the world is ready as evidenced by the fact so many people are awakening at this time. There are many people being inspired by a potential in their soul blueprints to connect with Gaia and ascend with her in this new accelerated reality.

Gaia's ascension has been in the workings for some time now, and if we look back on the various changes in every aspect of our reality including the shifts in our collective consciousness, it is obvious that there has been great movement towards a new human experience. This change began in small isolated pockets, but it is growing. We have the opportunity to experience a new unlimited reality if we just learn how to manifest it, and we will accomplish this with personal inner reflection paired with a desire to experience a higher vibrational living. This process was once a secret, hidden behind a veil of fear in order to limit us. The secrets of Universal laws and human potential were never discussed in our schools or open spaces. We were unable to move beyond because the wisdom and tools to ascend were denied to us. As a result, we continued to only live out the recurring story of limited expression as well as a stagnant progression and evolution. The power has remained with the chosen few and our progress has long been limited, but even the most insensitive were aware that something was shifting. There has been a quickening and even those who had little interest in spiritual awakening, still felt that 2012 was a pivotal year for heightened potential. This was a time when many of the inter-stellar and inter-dimensional restrictions and bans for outside help were lifted, and many UFO or lightship sightings promised a new dawn for future Earth. Prior to that, Earth had been left to its own devices in many ways, and being a planet of freewill and choice, there was not a lot that celestial and higher resonating beings could do to help move humanity in a more positive and loving manner.

Gaia set on a path of ascension and nothing will deter Her progress of this Universal plan from completing its cycle. The Universe, and even possibly other Universes, are likely structured in a similar manner, with a series of infinitely woven energetic systems, various levels of vibrational consciousness, and overriding themes that can be experienced, and all lovingly cradled under the auspices of the Creative Source. As one Universe, galaxy, or planet is in need of enlightenment, or a return to its core sacred potential, then a benevolent plan is set forth within the myriad of councils, beings, and groups that are assigned the responsibility for that particular system. Energetic and quantum systems that are threaded together by the rules and themes that its define its purpose.

This is one of the many Universal secrets and truths that has been withheld from humanity for so long, and ascension can allow us to open up in remembrance. Our spiritual capacity can encompass any area of interest, as our personal experiences up to now will determine what information and data we begin with. We will align who we are and what we know to the sacred frequencies by opening up at the heart level and allow new information to come forth. We are co-creating the new frequency that Gaia will slip into and this will allow us to manifest the lifestyle that many of us have wished for and intuitively known is entirely possible to experience. We are not alone, and we never have been. It is limiting for us to think that we are somehow the only life-supporting planet in our Universe or galaxy, and if we allow our awareness to expand and consider various levels of consciousness, vibrational existences, and life forms, we will see the infinite possibilities available to us.

Evolution, ascension, and expansion is the ability to access what could be and what may be possible, in order to allow our awareness and our consciousness to realize our expanded potential. These concepts allow us to grow and expand our understanding and create and activate new energy thus altering our entire physical and energetic body. We are not silent within the cosmos. Every thought we think and action we take reverberates throughout our Universe, and if we allow our vibration to be profound, loving, clear, and enlightened, then so too shall the energetic streams that resonate within Creation, be equally profound. We allow ourselves to become alive in a whole new way and how we interconnect with All That Is, and all life within it.

Ascension is the movement of what we are, multi-dimensional energetic beings, within our greater cosmos and the infinite and beyond what we ever thought possible. As humanity awakens to its place within the cosmos, and its power to ride alongside other ascended planets, like the Pleiades, we can begin to rebuild the corrupt systems and social structures that have held so many of us down for so long. It is in these awakening discoveries that each being will find their authentic voice and sing the song of the soul, allowing the spirit to bloom and rise again. With every thought, word, and deed, we co-create the new Earth glow that we all deserve to experience.

Join me on this ascension journey as we discover what personal and planetary ascension is really about and how to use the innate abilities that we all carry within to assist in creating new potentials upon Earth. We will tap into the multi-dimensional aspects of this reality and what being a multi-dimensional spirit essence means in the everyday life that one chooses to live. We will gain an expanded view and understanding for our planet, the galaxy that cradles us, and the Universe that carries us all as we learn to tap into the benevolence that enfolds us every moment of every day. Awakening and ascending is the process that brings us from one state of awareness to a higher state of awareness. These expansions, personal offerings through experience, and study into the gifts of our energetic Universe, you will see that there are great treasures and gifts for all who desire to access and claim them.

As the new Earth awaits, dear lighted-ones, join me in this exciting and profound journey, as we better understand the true nature of our reality today. There is so much to explore and discover on this path of ascension. As we open ourselves to the unlimited potential that awaits all of us, we will offer gratitude and celebration to the teams of beings and celestial family that have waited patiently for this time to arrive. As we grow into illuminated galactic humans, we will access sacred information that has long been hidden within us and we will create new opportunities for eventual communion with our greater cosmic family when we take our rightful place within the Universal family of light.

Chapter I

Introduction to Ascension

What is Ascension?

Gaia is alive and she offers Her own unique expression of purpose and desire to the Creator, as does everything else in existence. She desires to move away from an unhealthy state of imbalance and Her call for help has been heard by All That Is and Her ascension has begun. We not only live on and with the Gaia, but we are a part of Gaia.

Ascension can be triggered in a myriad of ways and whatever it was that triggered our unique expansion and self-discovery process, was designed to fit our precise evolutionary experience. The evolutionary expression that Gaia is experiencing is creating a great imbalance that is affecting all of creation, every planet, every galaxy, all Universes, and even the multi-verse. The One, the All That Is, has stepped in to bring about a resolution. That resolution is to implement Gaia's ascension plan. Gaia is awakening and as we are part of Gaia, so too are we awakening.

The awakening process triggers a greater understanding of our entanglement between all multi-dimensional aspects of who we are and how we are more than a physical body. We live within an energetic existence that moves with us, through us, and it beckons us to connect to it. Awakening inspires us to expand our awareness and know who we are in a grand benevolent ascension operation of wisdom, intelligence, love, and grace. What occurs within is all inter-connected and enmeshed with every aspect of the greater Universe and beyond. We are the consciousness of Gaia and of our cosmos. As we expand so too does Gaia and everything else in the Universe and beyond.

Life around us is changing, because we as a collective are changing. The more we tune-in to these energetic subtleties, the more we will notice that reality is changing. For those of us who have been on the path of ascension for some time now, we can physically feel the energy surges as cosmic alignments occur. We have attuned our physical vessels to move with these energetic alterations and shifts and sometimes these changes have been tumultuous. Even so, experiencing the physical symptoms of intensified ascension energies and streams we allow all dis-ease to be brought to the surface for release and healing is extraordinary. As humanity changes, shifts, and alters the energetic states of Gaia, we can see our physical reality changing to follow suit.

As we reflect upon the concept that we call time, we notice it is speeding up and we cannot physically keep up with it any longer. For many centuries, esoteric teachers have been teaching us that time is an illusion and if we, in our awakened state, let go and surrender our need to control these illusions, we will become aware of the true aspects of the Universe and the layers of energetic webbing that is the multi-verse in which we exist.

Ascension is remembering the innate brilliance we all have within us and feeling truth, rightness and alignment with a life that we desire. The ascended has embraced all aspects of their whole self, particularly those aspects that have been forgotten for a very long time.

There are countless stories, included in even our earliest scriptures that describe the experiences of people who have ascended. These tales include descriptions of dramatic physical transformations that were brought about by life-threatening or life-altering events, such as golden, glowing beings ascending from their physical forms. Those who experienced these things returned to a regular existence, but they were greatly transformed with new insight, wisdom, and knowledge. These people, in turn, chose to use their freewill to share their experiences and learning to assist others in achieving a similar state of enlightenment.

Today, it is not necessary to suffer though a life-threatening experience to begin the journey to heightened awareness and ascension. Awareness of All That Is, our cosmic heritage, and our place among the star families has always been our birthright and Gaia's ascension ensures that we are part of that Divine plan.

As we begin to ascend, we gain greater ability to understand what makes humanity unique through an expanded acceptance of what makes humans human. We exist as a physical, spirit energetic essence, in partnership with the guidance, benevolence, and wisdom of the Higher Self, Soul, and Over Soul, and we are fully entangled and enmeshed within the body of existence to serve the evolutionary process that is reflected back to Source and All That Is. This is what is meant by, "we are all connected" and "we are all One." Although it may appear that we are separate beings, we are ultimately connected in a profoundly refined and energetic manner. At the cellular level, we are as one, and as one being ascends, expands, and aligns with one's Higher Self, all within Creation has shifted with this change. This is why any change you make affects the All, and why the wave of awakening feels the way it does. There is a wave of humanity awakening and tapping into the expanse of Gaia's loving cosmic potential.

The process of ascension allows us to understand the magical essence of consciousness, so we can see that this physical reality and some of the constructs we exist within are really illusions. We will come to understand that all of our experiences, in any realm and in any star system, are for the energetic experience and the knowledge that experience brings. Once we move beyond what is really at play here, we can then use our inner wisdom, Universal law, and Universal energy, as well as divinely offered synchronicity, to truly create the life experience we ache for and thus adding to the holographic nature of Creation.

The ascension process allows us to slip naturally into the magical flow of the Universal stream of the infinite, All That Is, and Source of the infinite. As we slip into the natural flow of life, and let go of mundane struggles and self-limiting beliefs, we begin to flow in the elegant dance with Creation in the most magical way. This occurs when we shift our beliefs about what is possible and surrender into what has always been within us.

Trusting what is within and our link with Creation was an attribute gifted to us the moment we were conceived, and it will open us to the true historical heritage of humanity and Earth. There are profound creative potentials that humanity is capable of and in the coming years, we will see this as all aspects of our social structures and scientific innovativeness will move into the embodiment of its understanding of consciousness, and the unseen. We have seen tremendous awakening in the acceleration since 2012, and more and more groups and pockets of light are sprinkled all over the planet to assist with the amping-up of the collective vibration for such social changes to occur. All of these timely evolutionary shifts will lay the groundwork to ready the collective vibration, for the eventuality of open contact with our celestial friends and family. Human evolution is about expanding all that we are and explore all that we can be in all ways. Evolution, ascension, expansion, unconditional love, and benevolence is about inclusivity and Oneness with the all.

Ascension allows us to understand our greater place in the Universe, together with our ability to create and gain a clearer sense of who we are as a species. The energetic shift of even one person adds to the impetus to evolve and create a jewel among the stars that is our beloved Gaia. The great disconnection between humanity, nature, Gaia, Creation, and Source is due to old and limiting beliefs that we are separate, alone, unintelligent, and not of Divine blood. The disconnect between our physical existence and our spiritual being is the destructive tumour that has resulted in the economic and social catastrophe that poisons our existence. Fear creates limitation, hate, darkness, and separation which has resulted in the drastic and alarming damage, imbalance and extinction that stain our existence and our Gaia. We had forgotten our role as responsible stewards of nature, wildlife, self, our potential, and Source. These relationships are all entangled and connected, and should one aspect of this chain be darkened with disease, the entire system fails.

The Bigger Picture

For many years I have sensed that there is an underlying

plan, a Divine plan for Earth and this plan has been set in motion and is being watched closely by cosmic throughout the Universe, They are not just watching, some are actively involved with assisting in implementing Gaia's ascension plan. Gaia's ascension follows a similar pattern to the ascension of other planets and beings from those ascended planets are working to guide Gaia and us in our path to ascension.

I feel that there is a specific time line for this process and a scheduled set of profound changes will occur. Evidence of these changes and the greater expansion and Oneness are being felt and are manifest in the changes in attitude among the planet's population. We are beginning to care more deeply for Gaia and for each other as Universal unity touches the the hearts of all of us. This increase in compassion and benevolence are positively affecting Gaia and allowing for a more refined ascension energy to be present in our realm.

Understanding the core issues to humanity's challenges can allow us to bring light to the struggles and create greater harmony and peace for all. There is an energetic longing for spirit, for knowingness of greater light, the connection, the link, the entanglement that we have for our Divine and authentic self, and all of nature. We experience spiritual freedom and ecstasy in our dreamtimes, and higher consciousness states, where we are awake to our connection with All That Is. One of the rules we agreed to in entering this incarnational realm was that we had to forget our link with the Divine, so that the greatest aspect of growth could occur.

Ascension is living in the potential we create by shifting our core vibrations to fit our desired enlightened experiences. Ascension and enlightenment will eliminate the emotional defensiveness and confusion that are associated with our perceptions of limiting belief systems.

The Missing Link

As a planetary collective, we have been missing an integral ingredient that will enable us to survive and thrive in bliss with Gaia. We have forgotten that we belong to the greater whole, that we are loved unconditionally, and that we are supported with every step as Divine beings of Source essence and light. We have allowed a reality of technological devices, greed, and power over others, to replace that of the intimate human connection that our souls crave. This spiritual separation, emotional solitude, and lack of awareness has manifested as illness, aggression, and imbalance. This has been Gaia's painful story over our many lifetimes in which we have been working through a variety of lessons relating to our lower vibrational needs and wants.

We are all aspects of Gaia and She is an aspect of us. We are entangled and enmeshed and we are not separate from Her or any other aspect within Creation. Her state of consciousness is our state of consciousness, all the way out to All That Is. If one planet is being trampled upon, raped, and abused, then the entire system is out of balance. These planetary imbalances send warning signals out to Creation for a call of service and action. This is why so many star systems, beings, and angelic masters are coming to Gaia's aid. She is a beloved jewel within the greater cosmic system and the Universe is involved to assist Her and us in this monumental plan to help Gaia rebalance.

The Purpose

If we can lift our heads from all of our electronic devices for long enough to reignite our connection to life, we will be able to feel the love that has always been swirling around and within us. This is a gift from Creation.

In our highest state, we knew that awakening and moving with Gaia in remembrance and a new frequency would provide a experiences that simply could not be missed. It is in these experiences that love is truly found and in this depth of love for self, love for Creation, and love of Source, and Gaia, we re-ignite our purpose for incarnating in the first place.

This planetary ascension will activate our spirit to remember the grander aspect of not only who we are but all that we are entangled with. We are being invited to notice the potential to expand and take this realm to a new level of experience and resonance. As we grow in our awareness, we further our natural entanglement with nature, the animal and plant life, and all of Creation. Our celestial family draws ever nearer to our atmosphere because our collective vibration offers the frequency and potential for first landings.

First contact is not one that has to be amplified from the government's multi-billion dollar technology centres and sound detectors. First contact, and our desire and offering for communion, is offered to our refined personal resonance and how evolved we behave upon our own planet and with one another. This is how we ignite the birth of a new humanity as a co-creative member of our galactic community.

The expansion of our consciousness will allow us to coalesce with our Higher Self. This Earth reality is experiencing an upsurge in cosmic and Divine energy that will allow us to create a oneness, harmony, and unity on a planet that is, even now, teetering on the brink of disaster. Expansion is not only about moving beyond what we believe to be true, but it provides the inner clarity, knowingness, and self-love that offers an unlimited potential.

Acknowledge and embrace the brilliance that resides within, dear lighted ones, for your awakening is the nourishment of Creation. Your energetic imprint is like a pulsar of love and light that spirals through every part of this Universe. Transform every limiting and darkened belief that has kept us spellbound in fear, for each time you step up to your potential, you rise in united celebration with our infinite cosmos. Our celestial family awaits our embrace and as we ignite the love and light within, our newfound frequency vibrates and ripples through Creation.

Every lesson can bring forth a renewed desire to imbue all that we touch with a purity of intent and love. We, you, me, us, all have the potential to transform and ascend from any darkened depth.

We are ripe for a new adventure and our spirit is primed to love in a way that will allow us to truly tap into the brilliance that was encoded within us. We are alive, dear lighted ones, and now we can truly sense the colours and hues for all that love touches. There is no mystery, there is no hidden script, for the answer to whatever it is you desire to transform begins with the love you honour within yourself. Our potential, our purpose, our reason for being is the discovery of new heights and frequencies that we are able to expand into as we love with purity.

Love truly is the purpose of it all and it is the blood that runs through our Universal heart. Cast Divine love out to Creation and show the Universe your unique creative offering and you will have done all that you came here to do. Welcome to the 5th dimensional New Earth, dear lighted ones.

Our Divine Encoding

So many of us inherently know there is more to be discovered and we feel the ever-present energetic intensification that inspires us to come together sometimes by joining a group or an online platform and as we do we find ourselves in the presence of the masters and old souls. There is a power at work by teams of cosmic beings who are creating the synchronicities that so many others have written off as mere coincidence.

It is a divine plan to find ourselves in the company of people with whom we have so much in common, as well as an energetic compatibility. We feel an energetic pull bringing us together. These synchronistic events are the elegant design created on a much higher level and if we tune in to these events, we understand how enmeshed we are within this grand existence. We are the ones that are drawn to books like this, that allow us to feel something within, a stirring, a magnetic pull that speaks the urges that are left untouched within and beckon for their release. This is the Divine encoding within all that beats with the life that sustains us.

Within every cell, we have the chemical and geometric

design that is Source. When it is activated, the bond between all that we are (physical, energetic, and Divine) comes together and guides us through life like a profound machine that hums with precision as it picks up on all the things that honour the path that is lit by Source.

The Divine plan is for those that are ready to step into the Divine, to transition from living in a realm of limitation and pain, to one that offers potential for joy and prosperity beyond our imagining. Our purpose and our path, is encoded within us and it is activated when we answer the call of spirit. It will allow us to open to all that we desire, if we allow it.

We are encoded with the intelligence, the ability, and the potential of the Divine, and all the great masters that once walked this planet knew it. This is why they had the ability to spontaneously heal, transcend pain and even death, or manifest instantly by changing the molecular structure of physical items. The masters knew with every cell and heartbeat within their bodies that the Divine ran through them. With this level of knowingness, they were able to manifest anything.

I in them and you in me—so that they may be brought to

25

complete unity. (John 17:23).

As within, so without. As above, so below. (The Emerald Tablet of Hermes Trismegistus)

It is in these ancient understandings that we gain compassion for the path of others and allow their stories to unfold as they have designed, for all souls are unique and crave a myriad of expressions and experiences to arrive at the same awakening to Source. We are all created with the essence of the Divine and if we so choose to awaken into our unlimited potential, then we too shall walk as the masters walked.

As you awaken to the true depth and infinite aspect of your potential, you connect with your Divine and Source self, the highest aspect of who you are. Ascension is not just about the preparation for contact, or first landings, or even planetary healing, which are all valid, true, and real. At the soul level, we are moving through ascension to reunite into remembrance with our Divine aspect and the Divine aspects of Creation, or our return to more fully knowing Source.

We are Divinely encoded and we are known to the

Universe at large. We are infinitely surrounded, loved, and innately intelligent to master anything. If we allow our hearts to open, we will feel life and Creation for the first time. This is why people can be so moved when they are open to the love that can be felt when we know we are truly Divine beings of light. When we sense the love of self that Source has for us, you are forever changed.

Synchronicity

Synchronicity is a symptom of ascension and when you align with spirit and trust, in the most magical and unexplainable of ways, we will be shown that we are entangled. Synchronicity is our link and validation that we are entangled in such a refined way. Magical events will be shown if you open up to them and ask. You will meet who you need to, you will see what you need to, and you will be drawn to where you need to be drawn to for the answers you seek. Creation will always support benevolent evolution, always.

I am a seeker and the more questions I had, the more synchronistic experiences would flow to me. Being a super intense person, and somewhat of a micro-manager, the process of allowance did not happen easily. Allowance is key to creating synchronicity, creating contact, and any other ascension by-products. As we ascend, as we expand, there is more flow, more fluidity than ever before. Trying, making, or forcing things to happen are all attributes of old energy and lower vibrating realms. Allowance means you trust what unfolds. It is beneficial to allow the information and energetic gifts to flow to you with ease, grace, and honour as your Higher Self, your team, and the Universe is all conspiring for and working on your behalf.

As we refine our personal frequency, we literally lighten as physical beings. The faster our cells vibrate and move, the lighter we become. We become open, aware, and allowance becomes a part of our new behaviour mind-set. Allowance is the gateway for all of the magical gifts from the Universe to float into our lives. We merely need to align ourselves with our highest and most profound frequency and trust that whatever unfolds is in the best and highest interest for us.

Allowance and trust go hand in hand with the synchronicity that unfolds. Synchronicity is a by-product of ascension and it is the spiritual proof that we are in tune with our life's blueprint. Just as allowance and trust go hand in hand, so too does synchronicity and ascension. If you do not trust the Universal plan you have designed for this incarnation, if you do not trust your ability to create and align, you will not allow that level of potential to unfold to you. Synchronicity is equally matched to the level and frequency to which you align yourself within.

Synchronicity is a validation that our personal frequency is set at the right resonance. We can choose to create positive or negative synchronicity and as we create profound beliefs, let go of fear and doubt, and align with heightened qualities of Creation. The potential for powerful synchronicity becomes greater. Synchronicity the validation that we are connected with more than we can see. When gifts from the Divine float into our life, we experience a spiritual proof.

Synchronicity has a way to pull us to an awakened state, for how can such miracles unfold if there were not some more profound Divine plan of orchestration that we were entangled with? How could our lives be merely coincidental and accidental in our commingling? There are no accidents, and synchronicities will allow you to see how energetically linked we are with All That Is. Direct your frequency, direct your focus and definitions, and synchronicity will allow you to see where you sit. If you desire more profound synchronicity, if you desire to create a little magic in your life, or gain greater intimate connection and merging with all that you experience, then align to a vibration that will ignite this desire into action. Trust that all will flow to you and then watch what unfolds.

Synchronicity is one of the strongest symbolic reflections of our power to create. It is a tangible link to the quantum energetic world in which we exist. Synchronicity flows as we align with vibrations and see it reflected to us in the physical reality in which we experience. Synchronicity is unexplainable by most and yet floats into our lives with elegance and profundity. It allows us to acknowledge the help, support, and fairy-like guidance that is at hand in every moment. Synchronicity will always show itself if we align and acknowledge that we are the creators of it and desire it within our ever-changing reality. The more we trust and allow in our own innate abilities to interact with an unseen world of Universal energy and all the teams that support it and us, the more synchronicity will unfold for us. Embrace and honour the synchronicity that arises, for it will open the door to even more beautiful experiences. There is a cycle to all forms of energy and energy must always flow and move. As long as we are tuned in to what is being offered, synchronicity will allow us to see where we are resonating and how to better align.

I Am Affirmation

I am a creative aspect of Source. I am One with All That Is and all beings within Creation. My love, my light, and my intent will balance and heal all that I touch. I am One with All within Creation. I am supported, I am safe, and I am loved. I AM THAT I AM.

Chapter II

The Divine Plan

Everything in the Universe is energy. We are patterns of energy. One pattern is the soul, the Higher Self that is connected to All That Is. Another pattern is a spirit essence, the personality or self that was brought into this incarnation.

All patterns brought into your incarnation are aligned to carry out the plan that you designed for yourself for this life. This plan, this blueprint is an incarnational contract that you designed, includes a myriad of themes for you to explore during your life. The plan also outlines the help and guidance you will need and who will provide it to you.

There are no accidents in our designs. Even those who were born with extreme challenges have all chosen these themes for the purpose of soul's desire to experience expansive lessons. Life planning is done with all energetic circumstances taken into account at every level and what the soul desires for any particular incarnational realm experience.

There are teams of beings with varying skills, attributes, and frequencies to guide us in fulfilling our life plan. As we progress through the plan, different beings will step in at the appropriate time. It is important to know that we are never without Divine guidance or assistance.

A myriad of energetic parties, councils, groups, and spirit beings have aligned and benevolently communed in the planning, designing, and unfolding of your specific blueprint. Your blueprint is also aligned with the greater blueprint created for Gaia, the galaxy, and everything else that is the work of the Divine.

As you awaken, you will experience seemingly accidental or coincidental occurrences that occur with extreme precision and orchestration. This is the manifestation of the working relationship and entanglement of all our varied energies: our physical vessel, our Divine aspect, our Higher Self, or soul, with every other energetic vibration up to and including Source. Everything is working in a synchronistic grace of energetic waves imbued with intent and design, flowing forth through the expansive light from All That Is. We belong to a much greater family and it is filled with profound multi-dimensional beings with our highest and our best interest at heart in all ways.

We are powerful energetic beings entangled within a profoundly benevolent energetic field of potential. There are no accidents or coincidences in this way. There is Divine planning within it all and you are a powerful aspect within this beautiful design. There is a Divine purpose for your very incarnation, and setting sail on the tremendous experiential journey of ascension is possible, if you so choose.

Our presence here at this time is not an accident; we planned our placement here upon our beloved Gaia at this time so we can take part in this incredible ascension potential. We are here to experience something that few planets have been aligned to complete.

Be at peace and you will be able to feel your body shifting, aligning, and transforming to evolve with the ever-changing resonance that our planet is expanding into. Just know that there is nothing about our being here that is a 'chance circumstance or accident. Allow the Divine synchronistic gifts from Source and all within Creation, to show you the design, intent, and purpose for every life form.

You have chosen to be here, now choose to create the personal resonance that can carry all of us into a 5th dimensional frequency. You have the freewill to choose, but you cannot move forward until you form the intent to act. If you are truly ready for change, then expanding your awareness, expanding your very consciousness, is the key to enlightenment and ultimately ascension.

This time of awakening requires now more than ever that we trust that our path is a Divine one. This level of trust requires that you know you are a Divine creator and what you create in every moment can serve you.

Trust allows the free flow of Universal Divine energy to flow to you with an unobstructed view of your highest and best result. Your blueprint, your life plan, and your higher purpose are directly linked to the level of trust you have within. You will be intimately guided by this pull, the inertia that trust creates, to your higher alignment; love, fulfilment, and ascension, for these vibrations are the grounding elements of spirit.

Know that we have all chosen this exciting time with purpose and intent so that we cannot only assist in this process with Gaia, but also to be an example for other galactic civilizations who will learn from our experience.

Planetary ascension is a tremendous undertaking, and our collective readiness is approaching with a quickened pace as we act, think, and be the Divine essence that we were all created to be. It is with this pure knowingness that inspires reason and purpose in every living aspect, nature, wildlife, and every human being, as well as celestial, extra-terrestrial alien, and every other level of consciousness. Trust what you create, for it will always be reflected to you and realignment is within your freewill to alter and shift to ever-heightened states.

Whatever the story and blueprint is for your soul, know without question, without doubt, and with an unwavering sense of self that you are worthy of the life before you and you are more profound than you have ever been told. And even if an experience or situation may appear to be challenging or dark, it can unlock your grandest gift. Within every challenge is the lesson that brings you greater awareness, light, and potential to alter your path forever. You are a vital component in the Divine Plan and you do matter. Your blueprint is waiting for you to return with hope, insight, and the purity in which you entered into this realm of potential with. There is nothing you're not capable of achieving.

A Divine Plan has been written for each of us and awakening allows us to discover its details. As each successive energetic trigger is activated, we are enabled to amp up our resonance in preparation for the next level of integration and energetic offering. Our teams are always working and they are always nurturing and aligning for you all things possible, as you desire it. This is what is meant by being infinite beings of Divine light essence; for there is nothing that our light cannot expand to with the love and awareness, we choose to act upon.

As we awaken to and tune into all that surrounds us in this quantum brilliance of life, what we desire to experience will unfold before us as we align with it. All there is to experience in this lifetime is available and it merely requires us becoming aware of it, aligning to it, and acting to creating further potentials and expansion. This is how we are able to flow with Universal energy and when it all clicks, it all flows and your life will just work.

Cosmic Evolution

The planetary ascension for Gaia is of Divine planning and orchestration, which means that since the seeding of humanity long ago, there has been minimal evolution towards our greater spiritual potential and understanding of Creation, Source, and our entanglement with it. Spirituality and enlightenment were clouded in man-made, religious definitions, which are highly segregated, discriminative, and judgemental. These human constructs were created in ancient societies and use fear to control people. The experience of one's true spirit essence is quite the opposite of what we have been operating under for aeons. Spiritual evolution is freeing, unlimited, profound, and allows us to finally tap into our infinite potential within the All of Creation, and feel Source empowering us in the process.

This is essentially Gaia's turn in the path to celestial ascension and planetary evolution, as our greater cosmic family has been priming many of us for some time now, and we now align the with the frequency that can enable to create the vibratory 'landing pad' needed for safe and loving interactions, thus furthering our multi-verse expansion. We are all unique reflections and mirrors, not only for each other, but for other star systems, soul families, and the All That Is, to gain invaluable experiential knowledge from our experience. This is why it is said that, 'We are all One.' There is nothing that we do not think, say, or do that does not affect all that we are entangled with. Awakening, ascension, and expansion, allows us to see the inter-connecting sacred meanings of how and why we are as entangled as we are and how evolution is a natural part of our existence.

Other worldly contact is only a matter of timing, because expansion in these areas is no longer a matter of possibility, but eventuality as it is an aspect of cosmic evolution.

Evolution for humanity will move from being largely one that is an over-thinking and factually driven collective, to one that is synchronistically linked and able to sense, navigate, and create a new earthly experience. We will begin to intuitively know what is right, and we will know that the unfolding of what we create is part of the Divine design. As we consciously choose to take action with enlightened awareness, and powerful intent, we will create our highest and best life. It is in these every day actions and interactions that we will assist with the evolution and ascension of our planet and ultimately create our cosmic place within the stars.

Earth has progressed in many ways over the past half-century and she is on track with her transformational design into a new 5th dimensional frequency home. The change in our collective consciousness has been profound and it is hard to ignore how these awakenings are seeping into the mainstream of everyday life.

And just as the road ahead is not smooth for us, there are also growing pains associated with Gaia's evolution as she integrates both her and our evolving energies. Gaia will experience the smoothing out of geographical shifts that occur beneath her surface to remain in a constant state of balance. These smoothing out reactions can be seen as earthquakes, tsunamis, and eruptions, or other weather anomalies. Remember, we are pulsating energetic beings, and energy always must flow, and it is no different for a planet that serves and supports six billion plus people all resonating at varying levels.

But it will be worth it, both spiritually and temporally. This process of Gaia's ascension is one that should be enjoyable and as we awaken, as the old belief systems are shed, humanity will look forward with excitement and anticipation for the creative process to new socio-economic systems, which will flow and serve all people, not just the chosen few.

Human Truth

The truths of humanity and all of the stories of the great masters that walked this Earth in light will be unveiled to all those who desire to know. Our human heritage and our ancestral family will be brought to light so that we may finally honour their paths, truths, and wisdom. We will awaken the wisdom of our tribal ancestors who understood these inner shifts and offerings of Gaia and how She is entangled within Creation.

Those who are now awakening, and some who have been in the process of ascension for many years, have seen glimpses through to higher states of consciousness and seen astonishing truths. Our expansion, our growing awareness, will not only bring about new inventions and new social structures, but we will finally know the answers to all the questions about our existence. We will learn and

41

discover as energetic stories imbued with the unconditional love are revealed to us.

Not only will our cosmic understanding expand, but the geographical borders will shift to allow for greater freedom, abundance, and understanding for one another. Like a pulsar to the infinite, these energetic signals that are created as we expand into these infinite potentials for new Earth and the future humanity, ring through Creation with momentous melodies in celebration of our alignment with Source and benevolence.

Ascension and enlightenment is an ongoing process. Evolution will move in whatever direction it can, and change can be inspired from any form. Soon the whispers will no longer be whispers, and the calling will no longer be subtle. We are called to action by the need to know, and set the story, of who we are and what we are about, straight.

Our collective consciousness is shifting to an awakened state of potential that humanity is privileged to participate in. Humanity's rate of evolution and expansion of consciousness is directly equal to our desire to seek within, for going within is rising up.

Temporal Evolution

There has been great disregard for our planet and human life for eons. These atrocities have been our reaction and karmic bleed through from countless lifetimes marked by fear and limitation. But now it is time to dig deep within the essence of who we are and begin to heal all that no longer serves our higher vibrating core. We will now learn new ways to nurture our planet and rediscover natural ways to co-exist in harmony with all species on and off of our beloved Gaia. Light begins at home. As we create each day with light-filled intentions, loving excitement, and compassion for all, we expand our essence in monumental ways. This electromagnetic charge that we emit, from living in light and love, are pulsars that propel into the infinite and beyond. For remember, we live in an illusionary life swirling in vast amounts of empty space, and if this is the case, then we can truly create anything because it is all within.

All beings and species within our Universe are instinctively connected to everything else. Not only are the wildlife connected to Gaia, but so too are we and we are all affected by Her current state of imbalance and Her movement to rebalance and ascend.

As Gaia ascends and more of us join her, there will be a greater demand for temporal changes. The collective will demand cleaner foods, enlightened media, entertainment, social systems, and structures with greater integrity, because our reality is shifting along with us.

Wholeness and Oneness

In order to understand *wholeness*, we must first awaken and experience the Universal belonging within ourselves. This is a great paradox; we need to create our wonderland inside of us, so that we can experience it in the illusory external world. To do this, we must search deep within ourselves and discover the truth about why we are here.

This is a time for you to allow your light to shine forth -- the light that is within and has been within since the beginning of time. You have carried within you in every realm you have visited. This spark of light within you is a spark of the Divine Source. As you work toward your ascension, as you expand further into your Divine self, you will finally see just how brilliant you are in the eyes of Creation.

This process cannot be hurried. You are here because you have heard the call of the spirit that is offering you a greater understanding of the subtleties of Universal energy and its laws. Trust and surrender to the call and allow yourself to experience what is innately yours. Soon, you will truly experience the profundity of your existence. You matter. You are valid. You are magical. You are immense in this Divine plan, and you exist because of what you have to offer. How often have we been told that we are required, important, and valued in this life experience?

The power we have to create our life and reflect our brilliance back into the world is upon us. Awakening is a process of guiding our steps, and our breathing, and our thoughts, and that which we speak. All this is done to create a shift in frequency that defines us. This is our grand step forward for all of humanity. This is a grand step forward for you as you take this magnificent opportunity to step through the doorway and rise above all doubts and fears. The path will take us to a deeper connection with nature and *All That Is.* This is the fulfilment of our Divine promise and it is the key to profound happiness and joy.

This time of awakening and acceleration can give us the

opportunity to honour who we are, honour Gaia, honour our presence among the many multi-dimensional beings, and transform what truly is the event of the cosmos. We are a very powerful and creative species. This is a time to honour and embrace all that we are and as we redefine, and recreate the story of Earth, we alter her history forever.

As you read these words, the energy of Source is pouring forth and offering you the glimpse of what may be, so may you go from simply reading this, to digesting this, and then to integrating the essence of pure unconditional love for you from Source. You are on the path to the highest of realms. You are on the path to reconnect with Source, to become whole with Source.

Becoming whole once more is to experience the unfolding of your Divine-hood as quantum energy brilliance and feel your energy enmesh within Creation in a most profound and intimate manner. You will feel your way back into spirit remembrance and know with certainty your innate brilliance to transcend from one vibrational encasing, and consciousness state, to a whole new level of resonance. As you realize your Divine aspect, you will transform all that you are into what you were meant to be as outlined in your incarnational blueprint. We will become whole and one with *All That Is*.

Profound Godly essence resides within our DNA, like encoded brilliance, we only need to activate it for it to awaken and affect us in incredible ways. As you use your spiritual discernment, you will come to know that you have profound tools within to alter and shift everything you experience. This is the spark of Source and it resides within every cell of your physical vessel. These encoded aspects of our DNA are the Divine within our very cellular make up and in the years to come, scientists will be able to explain how our species is evolving, but many of us will have already ascended. We will have experienced this evolution first hand when we have physically become one with *All That Is*.

Through our choices, we will move onto the path to ascension. We will expand our awareness and naturally include all aspects of who we truly are and we will merge it into the experiences we desire. This process will activate our spirit essence to connect to the multi-dimensional quantum aspects of who we are and what we desire to be. This in turn will provide us with greater connection to the whole and infinite aspects of who we were created to be. And were created to be multi-dimensional aspects of Creation. We have within us the tools to effect this change, to expand, and we activate these tools with love and a desire for greater Oneness. Oneness will bring us greater health and greater capabilities to allow us to live in balance, peace, abundance, and infinite wellbeing. We will discover great potential, ability, and opportunities to tap into the infinite pools of wisdom, information, and youthful application that every spirit essence owns.

Transformation

Gaia's ascension is underway and her transformation is palpable. You may have felt a subtle difference in the world and in yourself. Do you feel more sensitive emotionally, physically, and intellectually? These are aspects of our reality inter-mingling with the energy of not only what we are, but who we are becoming. One of the most prevalent Universal lessons in the process of ascension is that we truly begin to fathom the aspect of our Oneness with all things within Creation. We are all entangled at the finest of energetic levels, and we are deeply connected to it all, as we exist within this dance of electromagnetic energy, we are affected by every change that is offered by this vast Universe.

As Gaia's ascension is in mid-point status, we're ever closer to gaining full access to our heritage, and all of the Universal secrets and understandings that have been hidden from us for so very long. Full consciousness is upon us and nothing will be omitted from this energetic makeover.

Social Transformation

Every area of our existence will be affected by this energetic insurgence of ascension energies. We can expect extraordinary archaeological and scientific discoveries that will offer an opportunity reassess our beliefs and history. Our political world is shifting and our economic policies will continue to transform to meet the compassionate and socially just expectations of a higher vibrating society.

Personal Transformation

As we ascend, our physical bodies will adjust to accommodate our new expanded thoughts and behaviours. Even without our active participation, we are already in experiencing an evolutionary change, as Gaia's energies shift under the direction and guidance of countless celestial teams. These teams stand ready to assist you in your personal ascension as well and as you spiritually change, you will also physically change. This is the alchemical process of ascension.

Each time that we expand our conceptual thinking, there are energetic triggers that occur within the pineal gland, and pathways within the brain open up. In these pulsations, we send out vibrations that desire the response and return frequency.

Chapter III

Gaia

Gaia's Ascension

We are all higher consciousness beings and we all have the ability to access higher states of awareness and find the answers to all of our life issues or dilemmas that are preventing us from living a fulfilling and love-filled life. When we begin this process of inner reflection, there is a celebration among the many higher beings of Creation.

Our awakening and our shifting consciousness will enable us to realize our potential to be powerful multi-dimensional creatures. And as we contribute to the vibrational resonance of the planet, Earth's resonance will grow and strengthen and ultimately touch others and inspire them to seek their own ascendance. We will all escape the limiting darkness and strife of the past and rise above to create light, balance, abundance, harmony, and a more entangled experience with all of Creation.

There are no accidents. There are no coincidences. We

create everything that we experience and I do not mean this metaphorically. This statement is meant to be taken literally. So many people are awakening now because there are powerful forces feeding this process, enabling an ease of access to the energies that help us connect with the sacred energies that are guiding us to ascension. Our potential to ascend has been multiplied exponentially.

If you are awakening now, in this planetary activation into a heightened frequency, you have the increased potential to stake your claim and really create a powerful, creative, abundant, and intimate life that is filled with excitement and miracles. You have the ability to create a new powerful life with every thought, every belief, and every action you take. How you align your energetic frequency in this moment, will directly equal what you experience, always. We came into this life with the abilities to manifest and create and they are within us right now.

The Divine plan for Gaia will allow all to create for themselves the potential to expand into a new way of living. We even see the intuitive brilliance in the genetic change in children born in recent years, and all new sparks and triggers that awaken more in the coming years, will add to the culmination of the planetary energetic story of Gaia's ascension. We are sitting in the middle of the most profound global acceleration, and it is all by Divine design. This process of accumulation of positive, loving energy, infinite potential, and seeking of light behaviours, will enmesh in such an entangled way and in every layer that planetary ascension to a 5th dimensional frequency will be the result.

Our planet is shifting to a new level of resonance in order to bring the highest aspects of Heaven down to Earth, for all to live in peace and harmony with all species, including planetary and intergalactic beings. It is a cosmic agenda, and many beings from many varying systems and vibrational frequencies, are in constant alignment with Gaia, working with her to ensure success. We have chosen, at our higher levels of consciousness, to be here in this time of great acceleration because we knew the profundity of the potential we could experience and we wanted to be a part of Gaia's re-birthing into a 5th dimensional frequency. It is Gaia's turn, and as divinely planned, she will return to her brilliance and stand boldly once again in this magical corner of the Universal sky, announcing her presence among the awakened. Those who chose this path are initiated into the awareness of Oneness within the whole, and realize the potential we carry to access the new higher vibrational energy and its associated thought and knowingness.

We live within certain Creation rules, just as other planets, realms, and star systems do, and each planet exists with its own specific set of rules. On Earth, we are an energetic collective body and everything we do, think, act upon, has an effect on the whole planet and all its inhabitants. We co-create experiential consciousness within our collective consciousness, just as we co-create with Gaia as she sits right now. We create based on our perceptions that are influenced by what we believe we are re-creating based on the lessons as we begin to experience the unveiled reality.

We agreed to experience the rules that govern this reality, rules such as, freewill, gravity, spiritual forgetfulness, imagination, and unlimited potential, etcetera. Freewill is a powerful tool, but it is one of the reasons humanity is currently stuck in forgetfulness and devolution. This is why cosmic, celestial, and inter-galactic beings and councils have been called upon to assist in Earth's awakening.

Prior to 2012, these beings were governed by strict rules of engagement with us that limited their contact. A call for help was sent out into the Universe from a suffering planet and its inhabitants to realign and re-balance Gaia's sacred energies. The energetic call was heard and received by Source or God, and in such a loving and benevolent system of light, no planet goes unnoticed and unattended. The call was heard and a cosmic plan for Gaia's ascension was set in place.

2012 marks a demarcation as it was an important cosmic transitions when the door was opened wide and all cosmic beings were given access to Earth, which further increased the relative volume of ascension energies on our planet. Earth's energetic shift and the access to our planet by otherworldly beings, has resulted in more paths and guides to those paths to move toward ascension.

Since the First World War, it has been obvious that this powerful tool of freewill, this luxury that we have been granted from Creation, has been seen as a free ride for those of lower vibrations who would use this tool to control and undermine our planet and our people, thus blocking our potential for a peaceful and abundant future. In many countries, those in leadership positions have been gotten very close to destroying Gaia completely. This is the call for help that caught the attention of many beings throughout our Universe who have recently stepped in, with loving and benevolent action, to become more openly involved in Gaia's renewed evolution.

These cosmic beings will assist us in preventing the annihilation potential of destruction and nuclear irresponsibility by intervening. They will stop and disengage any large-scale destruction device or agenda. They will protect us from the high level of disregard for human and cosmic life that is part of our collective human experience right now. Those who have begun the enlightenment journey know, as the cosmic beings know, is that we are all connected. A massive and horrific nuclear event on Earth would not only destroy life here, it has the potential to ripple throughout Creation on the multi-verse level and negatively affect life and cosmic stability in many other realms as well. Thankfully, we are Divinely protected. We live within the rules of freewill, but a concerted resolve of those who strongly desire an enlightened way of life will continue to strengthen Gaia and the frequency associated with Her and our ascension. The opposing vibration sent out by those who choose to remain in a state of disrespect and naiveté will be overcome, as the two opposing frequencies cannot continue to co-exist for long.

Since the inception of civilization on Earth, Gaia has been protected by the highest of light beings in our Universe, as mandated by Source. Look at our history, and even the current news programs, and you will see countless tales of battles fuelled by greed and entitlement to Gaia's abundant resources. The constant dissent about religion, beliefs, and social status and who is more entitled to land and resources is devastatingly negative. Every incarnation is an opportunity to work through such limitations and rise above them, to strive toward enlightenment. We always had this potential, even in past incarnations, but the current planetary shift had multiplied our potential for success. We have an abundance of energy to enable us to overcome the fear that binds us, and all humanity, in this deadly dance of limited options that must become – and will become—a part of our distant past. We will evolve to a higher state with the assistance of the growing energy of Gaia and the guidance of the newly arrived cosmic beings. We can use our freewill to choose to live in a state of love, harmony, and peace because we know that these changes will manifest a new life experience for us and they will contribute to a harmonic and peaceful planet that is open to cosmic invitations of love and light.

The scales are tipped in the favour of ascension, and there are enough of us desiring, seeking, and acting with light within, that a profound energetic surge has propelled us in a new and fresh way particularly since the catalyst of 2012. The catalyst, the climax, and pinnacle of planetary ascension, is in full motion. We are imbued with a new sense of hope and potential for what lies ahead as we create brilliance in this now moment. The question of the millennia is, how will this all unfold and are you ready to tap into the potential within?

Now that planetary ascension is upon us, there are an increasing number of wonderful resources being created with a conscious intention to help us focus on *how* to live more fully in the *now* so that we can reap the benefits of a blissful life. In living in the now, we are connecting with our ability to flow into the presence and the essence of pure knowingness and Light. Enhancing, expanding, and exploring the infinite aspects of consciousness is the mastery of reflecting all energetic experiences, downloads, and symbolism, in the now. This Divine stream of energetic fluidity, this infinite web of knowledge, wisdom, abundance, joy, bliss, and so much more, is accessed in the presence of the *now.* As we reflect upon what is being mirrored to us in these experiences, we further stimulate the wisdom and light within us. It is in this seeking that expansion occurs and with expansion, comes ascension.

Our own ascension is facilitated by Gaia's ascension and as she transforms, our won transformation becomes easier. However, for Gaia to ascend, we must ascend. Her land, her polluted waters and soils are directly related to our state of mind and our collective consciousness. If we hold ourselves in low regard, then this energetic vibration is mirrored to our planet.

As we pollute and disregard life or ourselves then there must be an energetic reaction or response. All things within Creation desire balance. The state of our planet is what is being mirrored to us so that we can awaken to our personal states of being and attempt to make a course correction. Our celestial friends and family have an over-riding plan to assist us if we have not cleaned up and changed for Gaia's survival affects not only humanity, but her ill-health ripples to all corners of Creation.

Planetary Awakening

It is doubtful that anyone can actually predict how our planetary ascension will unfold. Gaia is a planet that operates on freewill and there will be some that are simply not be ready or did not agree to ascend in this incarnation. However, it is also likely that Gaia's shift into the 5th dimension is a matter of years, not decades. We have been wandering around a maze for so long, but now we can glimpse a glow showing an exit from this darkness.

We are awakening to an immense power with a huge potential for a massive ascension of all of us and this is known as our world is exhibiting a significant frequency shift as so many awaken and bring about significant changes in our worldly experience.

Not everyone on Gaia will tune into the messages and channels of potential and light. I am but one light-worker in a world of six and a half billion people although there are increasing numbers of those who seek light and live in the name of light. It is a veritable wave of awakening as so many activate their encoding to ascend. They crave the experiential path that frees their soul and awakens us to a pure knowingness of our unlimited potential and the love and Source essence that beats within us all.

This is ascension, dear lighted ones, and this is how ascension occurs at the planetary level. It starts within and one person at a time is triggered to create and traverse an ascension path of refining our vibration to one that incorporates infinite potential, love, and honour of self. This is our path, this is our ascension, and it is our will and intent that will create any outcome and manifestation that we know to be true for each of us.

The energy from one pure act of loving intent floats throughout the collective and out to the cosmos, and then soaks within the soils and waters of Gaia. Ascension occurs in one thought, one word of love, and in the eyes of those you meet.

We are each becoming illuminated humans that will soon move beyond the atmosphere and into the cosmos with our inter-galactic neighbours. Our physical bodies will adapt to these ascension energies and as long as we are clearing and releasing our limiting beliefs, the transition should be smooth and painless. Every aspect of us and Gaia will be affected and we will even begin to see, hear, and feel things entirely new. We will feel our skin tingle and vibrate as our cells and chakras move into high gear and our world will become a lot bigger as we begin to sense the presence of profound beings that walk with us every day. They will be reminding us of our innate abilities to sense our way through this profound experience and know that we are more than we originally thought we were.

Why Now?

Why change? Why all this talk about awakening and ascension, and why now? Those that work with light and focus on positive intent and action have noticed that powerful surges of energy have been gifted to Gaia and have taken this as a call to action to create an environment for the potential awakening of everyone around them. Even those who have not yet awakened can likely sense these powerful changes, particularly the profound essence of love that emanates from Gaia.

Love is the most powerful vibration in the universe and as we allow our own inner light to emanate, we strengthen the frequency for those around us. The light we emit touches and changes everything and everyone in our reality. Every tiny bit of light will have a profound effect on the darkness, particularly as it joins with Gaia, increasing the overwhelming benevolence and love that emanates from Her.

I feel, as many others do, that the time has come for humanity to step out of the dark and rise up into a new enlightened potential. Humanity has been held back by a veil of limitation and darkness, for much too long. The veil has shrouded our perceptions of our infinite potential. 2012 was a powerful turning point in Gaia's energetic path to ascension.

Gaia's core frequency has been slowly and steadily awakening over the last few decades. More recently, however, there has been a quickening, mostly due to the vast number of people opening, awakening, seeking, and remembering their Divine spirit potential. As more people awaken, there is more energy stimulating the awakening of others. The massive movement of energy is gaining momentum and everything is changing -- Gaia, her people, and even the cosmos.

A real shift is occurring causing a profound alteration to our collective consciousness. Humanity is becoming self-organizing, harmonic, and abundant as ascension energies are so abundant and inspiring so many people to seek greater understanding on concepts of self-empowerment and self-confidence. The potential for political and economic balance for all humanity is truly achievable. These amazingly subtle energetic movements are stimulating our collective consciousness and awakening so many and inspiring the creation of something truly magical and spectacular for Gaia and humanity.

But there is still so much work ahead of us to create strong vibrations and energetic portals in order to facilitate the mass ascension of humanity. We have help though as the most high celestial beings have been directed to intervene on our behalf and assist in this ascension.

A spiritual awakening will result in an ability to manifest anything, even more money so that we can buy more things. The greatest lesson that we will learn, however, is that our intimate link with Source will move us to use our gift to manifest for the higher purpose of helping Gaia. Our higher purpose is to live with spiritual intent and Oneness. Earthly possessions and titles will pass away but our service to Gaia's evolution and the salvation of humanity will remain with us forever. As we learn and then teach how to live in peace with nature, Gaia, and all of existence; we are helping to create a healthy balanced planet and the species that can take our place among the cosmos and our star families.

Gaia has suffered but now it is the time to set everything to right. The game of incessant greed and control that has seen humanity on the brink of destruction several times over has run its course. Creation's desire to see humanity experience the joy, bliss, and unconditional love for Her home, nature, and one another is the catalyst to Gaia's ascension plan. There has been a tremendous disconnect with nature and the human potential for generations, and this behaviour has diminished the balance of Oneness as well as Gaia's health and wellbeing. It is finally time for us to act to transform lower vibrational energies into lighted pockets of great human potential. We need to expand our awareness and tap into our spirit essence and eliminate the darkness, the negativity, the constraints, the restrictions, and limiting beliefs that have suffocated humanity for so very long.

A primary tenant of Universal Law is that everything must change, and in our planetary evolution, we are now ready to break free and create new ways, new systems, and new ideas that can provide us with a new perspective as we expand our level of awareness. We know that many will not choose to begin their ascension journey and contribute their personal resonance to the strengthening of Gaia and that is all right. At this time, because of divine intervention, the Gaia's ascension is assured and even the light of a few will the powerful enough to assure individual enlightenment for those who have undertaken this journey at this time.

Those that have entered this new quantum web are bringing light where there was once dark, and hope will replace dismay. We will bring our Universe together in a loving entanglement of enlightenment for ourselves, but most importantly for Gaia.

Healing

The spirit of Gaia is alive and well. She is home to many light workers and elementals that reside within the trees, the grasses, the mountains, and the water. As you awaken to the potential within, you will sense greater multi-dimensional energies around you even without being in a meditative state. This is a natural progression in the process of energetic expansion. Every physical element that

Gaia produces, whether within the animal or insect kingdom, cetacean or plant life, has consciousness at some level. There is energy and life in all things, and as we expand our consciousness, we will begin to tap into other states of consciousness all around us.

Nature is a gift that allows us to practice honing our innate abilities. Nature walks in the forest, or along beaches, or in gardens, can all inspire greater communication and communion, not only with your Higher Self and spirit guides, but with our loving Gaia. Allow yourself to slip into nature and pay attention to what you sense, what you hear, what you see. As you do this over time, you will experience your abilities to hone in to the more subtle forms of life that have always been amongst us.

Historically, we have disconnected from all things that are energetic and of natural design, and Gaia has been the one presence and gift from Creation that we have dishonoured and disrespected in horrific ways. Nature is and always has been the energetic environment that sustains us. Gaia supports us, nurtures us, and nourishes every aspect of life we exist within. She has the potential and offering to bring us in alignment with the Universal web of Creation, and yet we allow these offerings to pass us by. Awakening brings us the alignment and awareness of such profound gifts that have laid within paths we walk, and the food we eat every day. Nature is teaming with life at every level and we are here to reengage and entangle ourselves within these healing offerings once again.

A Meditation Exercise

I use a wonderful visualization in my daily meditations, so feel free to use this to tap into the nature energy offered by Gaia to propel and inspire you. Once I am grounded and centred, I visualize the spirit essence of who I am. This could look like anything to you, so be creative. I see a golden white spiralling ball of iridescent lights, swirling and linking energetically with the trees, the grass, and the air I breathe.

Visualize the textures of everything you can conjure that Gaia creates for our delight. Feel, see, smell, the various textures in your scene: the bark, the colours of the needles, the wind, the scent of the flowers, and the crisp flowing water in a nearby stream. Feel the branches as they tickle and enmesh with our spirit essence and feel your core vibration rise in frequency to match Source. Visualize your glowing essence merging with the elementals in the soil or the air or the water burbling over the stones.

Visualize your spirit essence, a beam of glowing light being filled with God's love, powerful and profound as it merges and entangles with you and the nature essence you have danced with. Imagine it spiralling, swirling, and igniting the Divine within you and see it expanding with every breath. Soak in the unconditional love and support that you are offered in these energetic entanglements and allow your Divine essence to be enmeshed with all nature consciousness that supports your life in this reality experience.

Visualize your essence being grounded into Gaia, like strong roots of an eternal tree, and feel her healing touch as her essence connects with your own. Breathe Her in and feel Her energy further grounding your essence into Her rich soil. Become One with Gaia and all that supports Her, and all that She supports.

This powerful nature visualization can heighten your connection and link with all of nature. As I stated earlier, our link and connection with Gaia has been a profound missing link in our ability to expand and ascend because we have believed that she is separate from us. Now we can consciously choose to reignite the desire to unite with all that Gaia is and all that She offers to humanity. We are entangled with and evolve within all that She is and offers to us. Play, dance, engage, and breathe in the light, the offerings, and the gifts that Gaia and all nature has to offer, for we are an aspect of it.

Trees offer wonderful and profound symbolisms and healing potentials, as do all nature beings and species. As you open and align your energetic field, you will find yourself attracting a variety of animals, animal spirit totems, elementals, and other forms of our multi-dimensional beings into your reality. Allow yourself creative playtime with the many energetic aspects that reside upon Earth, and as you do you will experience incredible healing energy that will be created. What most fail to realize, is that if we act as One with nature and all that Gaia offers, we bring ourselves as a collective and planetary species back in balance within our galaxy.

All of these playful interactions create potent and lasting energetic healing that can further strengthen and align our link with Gaia, Creation, our Higher Self, and our celestial team. This visualization will enable a deep connection with Gaia, but even if one chooses not to visualize oneself in a happy dance with nature and Her gifts, we must be aware of the necessity to, once more, engage, honour, and appreciate Her with heartfelt love and intention.

We have the potential and ability to create any visualization for ourselves with profound symbolism and emotion that is geared and synchronized specifically to us. We can ask our team for guidance in this way to assist in aligning us with our highest and best path and it will be given.

The more we commune and entangle with all nature; all animal species, the elementals, cetaceans and so on, we expand within the potentials that humanity has for greater expansion and learning. All life, all levels of consciousness, and all wildlife and beings are valued and honoured within Creation. We are entangled with every aspect within our reality.

What ails our planet, ails the soul of who we are. We are linked and entangled. If we live in respect and honour of life upon Gaia, we will be able to extend our understanding to life beyond our atmosphere. The question we could ask ourselves in these self-reflective moments is, "Would you approach a planetary species if they disregarded their planet and life upon it the way in which humanity has?"

Chapter IV

Awakening

Welcome to the Light

We are spirit beings and many of us are awakening to an inner light that is encoded within us. This awakening is often triggered when disharmony and daily frustrations inspire a deep desire for a better way of doing and being and we begin to search for this better way. Usually that search begins with books, classes, or group work. It will not take long before you begin to notice that you feel different. Your beliefs about life will then begin to change when your old beliefs feel outdated, negative, and fear-based and you will be filled with an even stronger desire to seek answers to explain your ever-changing reality and sense of being. Was it your inner voice that directed you to this book to find an answer? You are answering the call to understand your life's purpose and to align yourself energetically with the Divine vibration. Your desire is good and you are a worthy Divine being of light and the answers you seek are inside of you.

When I started this path more than eight years ago, there was not a lot of available information describing or explaining the sensations that were developing within me. I spent days at the computer searching for guidance but my search was quite frustrating as the answers I sought eluded me. Eventually I realized that I was searching in the wrong place. I had to find the answers within me; I needed to allow my higher self to explain what was happening deep in my soul. The insight that I needed was inside of me.

Insight is a greater understanding of our purpose and the powers that are present to aid us in that purpose. Insight, what a wonderful word — the word itself tells us where this knowledge and understanding lies. The exhilarating path of transformation that leads you to your true and divine self is within you and you will find it through a process of self-reflection.

As you seek the answers within, you will begin to experience an energetic or physical response as answers are revealed to you. You will experience a sense of familiarity when you realize that you always knew these answers. And as you take the time to reflect, contemplate, absorb, and integrate these answers, you will find you have been initiated into a heightened state of awareness and you have begun the process of moving forward toward ascension.

This is a grand opportunity to seek, enquire, and heed the answers that will bring you greater insight, greater expansion, and your ultimate evolution. Your incarnation on this planet at this time is your opportunity to learn these truly powerful lessons, to transcend the limitations of traditional thought and create the life that we truly desire and deserve. In this age of awakening, many souls will manifest events and circumstances that will enable all of us to awaken to the gifts within us. And as our soul stirs, we begin to create a world that can shine brightly.

The act of seeking marks the initiation to your path of awakening that can ultimately lead to ascension. It is your first indication that life should be better, richer and hold greater intimate experiences that make us feel fulfilled and excited. Life should be loving, intimate, full, honest, and exciting in every way. Life should be creative, joyful, inspiring, harmonic, peaceful, and enlightening. If life is any other way, it is because we have allowed ourselves to buy into, accept, and integrate limiting and/or negative beliefs.

Fear is the foundation of all limitations and it is what has kept the veil of illusion between us and our highest potential.

Modern science has shown us how negative beliefs and emotions damage our minds and bodies. Imagine, then, how fear is hurting our higher consciousness, that part that is a part of the energetic cosmos, a part of Gaia and all that is within her care. Fear inhibits the infinite potential of what is possible. Fearful beliefs are the catalyst to limiting emotional behaviours, such as worry, negative self-dialogue, negative definitions, physical and emotional stress, control, aggression, and so on. To resolve our issues with fear, we need to have the courage to bring all that haunts us into the light where what we fear can be examined, acknowledged, and released.

If you tune in to how you feel, what excites you, and what brings fear to the surface so you can address it, then eliminate it, then you will find you have tuned into a treasure trove of sacred and profound knowledge that the Universe is offering to you to reflect upon and use to alter your own life and the life of all of humanity, through Gaia. As you integrate this knowledge and wisdom into your daily life, you will discern your connection to the energy that binds us and is us, and is Gaia, and is the Universe. In your discerning state, you will see how every change that you make, even the tiniest of changes, will inspire a transformation in the Whole. As you open up and align to higher vibrations, you change everything — yourself and everything connected to you, which is everything that exists.

What has this life allowed you to learn? How do you envision your perfectly balanced world and what must you change, alter, or shift to ensure that what is being mirrored back to you is a reflection of love and light? We ask these questions so that we can propel ourselves toward self-clarity and moments of inspiration and insight as we seek after enlightenment. It is important to remember, our dear-ones, self-reflection is about self-discovery, not about blame. It is about owning your state of resonance and allowing yourself acknowledgement, love, and the ability to move beyond this moment and realign to a higher frequency. We have, within us, the innate power to create anything, but we cannot change what we do not own. Be bold and be clear about what you desire. This will allow you to start aligning to the essence, to the vibrations that bring you excitement, joy, and love. The process of Ascension is mechanically simple, but it requires that we be honest and thorough in facing our fears. It is important to ask yourself the tough questions and face the answers head-on. Only good can come from being honest as you access the light to enable change and ultimately, Ascension. Honest self-reflection will help you discover new truths about yourself.

Once we have begun this journey of self-discovery and self-reflection, we will begin to see miracles unfold, our state of being will expand and become lighter, and knowingness will replace limiting doubts. As a human collective, we will access ancient systems of knowledge and wisdom, and we will be reborn with fresh new eyes to see and sense our potential. The introduction of these new elements will bring about an alchemical process; the aspect that we are now will transforms and transcend into a new heightened state of light resonance.

As we become aware of what is possible, then we will begin the process of aligning our energy to the types of experiences that we truly desire. This process shifts us into a state of ownership of what we are and what we will become. There is nothing that we cannot create when we take on the power associated with this ownership. We are, in fact, merely taking back the power that we have always had at our disposal to direct our lives and the evolution of our souls. As we embrace who we are, with all of our human faults and mistakes, and fall back in love with Creation, Gaia, nature, and ourselves we will align ourselves with our Higher Selves and Source. This alignment will allow the co-creation of a new 5th dimensional existence. Are you ready for this journey?

We do not need to create elaborate systems and processes for enlightenment to occur, for the mechanics of ascension are truly simple. You will discover that you always manage to manifest what is right for you in every moment. As you read this, there are energetic vibrations being activated within you. As these energies imprint on your soul you will sense a portal opening and providing you access to ideas and inspirations to guide you on your higher path. You will be provided with cues, clues, and gifts to enhance our potential for greater intentional living as you open yourself to the promptings of your higher self.

You can facilitate this process by engaging in simple expansion exercises such as reading books like this and meditating on the messages on the pages. The Universal web of consciousness will work work to guide you to the discovery that we are all an integral part of something great and wonderful and once we realize it and feel it, the sense of belonging will make us feel whole.

Awakening

Several years ago, I experienced a life-altering event and as a result, all of my 'soul-searching' questions were brought to the forefront for exploration and discovery. Like many others in the awakening process, I remember many moments throughout my lifetime where the energetic cues and symbols were offered to create opportunities for me to seek, connect, and link in a much deeper way. The more that I discarded and ignored what was being offered, the more profound and dramatic the triggers were. Like most people, I carried on without further investigation, and labelled such magical experiences as 'coincidence.' It wasn't until I was in my late thirties that I had the maturity and ability to understand that all of the 'coincidences' were a much higher calling to a path that I now reside in and have fallen in love with.

Awakening occurs to provide us with the opportunity we

need to experience how intimately linked we are to *All That Is*. Awakening occurs at the soul level. The soul will manifest activations to your Higher Self, your spirit guides, and then to your celestial team, who will step up in action to fulfil items within your life contract. The Most High directs these stages of activation. Your team will launch energetic cues, symbols, and clues to guide you and bring you in alignment with the desire to know more, be more, and feel more. And so the path to enlightenment begins.

Awakening allows us to open to our authentic self. We can let go of feeling obligated to act in a certain way to please others, or compensate for others' unhappiness, because we can sense there are emotional issues not being discussed or brought to the forefront. Empaths and psychic intuitives do this without really knowing and then feel exhausted and overwhelmed, and will use anything to mask their authenticity and hide forever in the sleepiness of denial. For when we have been authentic, we have been judged, shunned, and ostracized. We tell people we are fine, when we're morbidly unhappy and disconnected, and we look to anything to fill the void of our disunion and detachment from Spirit and Source. These are all a part of the natural process of self-discovery in the awakening process, for there are times we have to reach despair before we rebound into bliss.

In the process of awakening, and as you become comfortable with your unfolding innate skills and abilities, there may be experiences when you are sensing something and you will be told or taught something totally different. It is important to trust what you are sensing, for your intuition is never wrong. Your intuition is linked to Source, to Creation, to Gaia, and it feeds you energetic information so you can fulfil your desires. While the rest of the world catches up energetically, you may need to learn how to balance what you perceive to be true, and what you are being told. Use this as an opportunity to enhance your capacity for compassion and understanding. Just know that the world will change and soon will match what you perceive. Stay true to your path, and hone what you sense. If you ask for validation from your celestial team and spirit guides, and if you ask for clarification, know it will always be given.

Awakening will stir us into action. When we are tired of lack of meaning, depth, and intimacy, we will begin to seek a deeper sense of living. Humanity has tended to wait until the darkness hovers before change is really created and we no longer have to take this approach for a harmonic experience. We have the power and strength to rise above any limitation and feeling of lack. We are shedding centuries of habitual energetic numbness and darkness, so awakening will take time. Despite this, there is perfect timing to everything within this brilliant and profound dance of glorious Universal orchestration. We live within an energetic web and it is always moving, changing, expanding, contracting, and we are alive with it as it is within us. We are entangled, dear lighted ones, and awakening is our remembrance of this graceful dance.

Awakening can start out quietly and with great subtlety, and ascension triggers can be ignited in the form of whispers, tugs, pulls or situations to jar you into noticing something is shifting. Sometimes it is merely to notice the beauty of a rainbow, the brilliance of a flower, or the perfectly coloured patterns on a wild animal. The Divine life essence within that allows you to see, sense, and feel your deep connection with all else in the Universe, and it can really be this simple and this beautiful, for nature has always been our greatest teacher and her lessons are undeniable. Gaia is constantly and unconditionally gifting us with her presence of nature, nourishment, and beauty, and if we listen, if we stop and notice, there are synchronicities that can allow us to tap into our multi-dimensional profundity if we let it. She allows us to endlessly peek at Creation in the most profound of ways and she then allows the moments of awe to ignite our passion to love and reconnect with life before us. We are so blessed for her offering in our path of awakening and ascension, for it brings us to our most expansive self. All it takes is our natural ability to tune in to what is always around us and within us.

Global Awakening

The world is awakening. Earthly change does not require that the majority believe in what is actually happening. Even if the majority of people choose to ignore what is happening, or pretend it's not happening, it will have no bearing on Earth ascending. However, this global awakening is inspiring more individuals to awaken.

There are so many experiencing calls through their dreams, visions, and some even experience visitations. Gaia will ascend into the footing of the 5th dimensional field where she will enjoy a perfect state of balance. This energy acceleration is seeping into every part of our daily life. There is no doubt that things are changing. A world of unseen magical occurrences is revealing itself and it can no longer be ignored.

Chapter V

Freewill and Choices

Atlantis

Long ago, conflict arose in the city of Atlantis. The city inhabitants were the warders of a set of sacred crystals that enabled the people to manifest as higher beings. Sadly, a faction arose from this otherwise peaceful society. This faction, known as the Sons of Belial, were motivated by greed and lust for power and they sought to control these crystals.

The Sons of the Law of One were tasked with working with the crystals, with respect, love, and reverence of the crystals power, to heal and to keep life on Gaia in balance. The Sons of Belail were jealous of the Sons of the Law of One, and they sowed seeds of dissension and Atlantis began to rumble with fear and disconnection.

Eventually, the Sons of the Law of One were infected with fear as they realized the devastation that could ensue if the Sons of Belial gained control over the sacred crystals. The

Sons of the Law of One knew what would become of their civilization if the crystals were not used with purity of intent and integrity and so they created a plan to safeguard what they could.

The Sons of Belial wanted control of the crystals for they feared that the resources, their ability to manifest at whim would be lost and these negative beliefs were the core temptation that spurred on the devastation that rippled through the Universe. Atlantis is just one of humanity's earliest cases where fear based beliefs spawned ideas of power, greed, and control, and ultimate destruction of all that existed in one of our most advanced civilizations. Even as advanced as Atlantis was, fear crept into the belief systems that directly affected their perceptions, their reality, and ultimately their freewill to choose to see beyond their imagined limitation and create balance and fairness and peace for all. As fear began to separate these two factions, the lower energy vibrations created by the Sons of Belial caused a great instability and eventually the sacred crystals were affected and Atlantis was destroyed.

The destruction of Atlantis not only affected the people of that time period, but it altered the landscape across our planet as Gaia was beset by massive tsunamis, earthquakes, eruptions, and many other devastating cataclysms. These rang so deeply that shifts occurred in her planetary grid and her energy centres contracted. A veil of illusion fell over all humanity, even those that carried the Akashic memories. Since then, we have been unable to see what we are truly capable of since those harmonic times of early Atlantis. Our incredible creation abilities, insight, peace, and balance were destroyed because of fear and greed.

An energetic veil has covered humanity ever since Atlantis fell into the depths of the Atlantic. The mass disregard for life, the mass loss of peace, harmony, and blatant disregard for all that was sacred, created all the limiting belief systems and its associated lack of connection between each other and every other entity.

This veil was created by our collective energy, but despite the blindness it will allow us to explore our creative potential as individuals and work toward stepping up our vibrations to match the frequency in which we can truly appreciate, understand, and respect the powers that we were gifted so very long ago. Once we ascend into a higher vibrating realm we, and all humanity will once again enjoy the intelligence and sacred knowledge that is currently hidden behind the veil.

This is the remembrance that we are awakening to. Fear breeds emotions and behaviours of control, aggression, negativity, corruption, deceit. Regardless of what beliefs you hold within you, there is always an opportunity to bring them to the surface and realign to a heightened state of awareness, thus allowing for a heightened potential and outcome. The fall of Atlantis is one our planet's most powerful lessons in the experience of believing that we are separate from Source and what that belief brings us to evolve into. If we truly understand in our awakening that we are never separated, we are always One, and we are intimately linked and connected to every other being in Creation, then we have no need to take from another, or control over another, and we begin to manifest systems that serve and benefit the All.

Freewill

One of the greatest gifts that we have been given as humans is the power to choose. As stated earlier, we have chosen to experience this grand planetary ascension, our evolution, and everything we experience within it. All incarnation experiences on the Earthly realm can be viewed in this way for it is a rule that governs this realm.

We are not forced to walk down this path of awakening and transformation. Each individual can choose and as a collective, more people are choosing to be more aware of the darkness and all the limitations, all the misconceptions about our heritage, governments, and the many missing links about who we truly are and why we are here. We are learning how to tap into our intuition, our creative imagination, and play with our infinite consciousness to experience Divine blessings in every day. In allowing our natural state of Divine spirit to emerge, we see new manifestations unfold. We experience new, higher ways of thinking, of being, and we are even inspired to create new systems to benefit all people, all species and once again, allow us to live intimately connected as a powerful community of light and potential within the vastness of *All That Is.*

Many people take freewill for granted and because of historical conditions, we have never truly realized the potential that we carry within us as a Divine human race within the loving arms of Creation. The evolution of humanity literally relies on our ability to choose. All physical beings choose at some level, at some state of consciousness to continue and evolve. The intrigue to move beyond and explore is what allows us to wake up every day and feel more than we did the day before.

Do you trust what you create? Do you trust that all that unfolds upon your path can benefit you in some way? Do you know that anything that may unfold can serve you and honour you in some way? Freewill offers to us the power to choose any vibration we desire. In your expanding awareness, you will rediscover these Universal laws and how you have every ability, skill, and potential to create a sense of peace, balance, and harmony. You own these sacred truths, dear lighted ones, and you open the portal to your own Divinity every time you redefine in light and choose in alignment with your heart's desire.

Many beings will choose not to ascend in this plan of progress for Gaia. In general, the masses may not be at the appropriate levels in order for all to ascend this time around and that is fine. All paths are valid and required for creation to experience the mirrored state of all choices. Ascension will always be an option and some souls are required to follow their blueprint and learn certain 3rd dimensional lessons and realities before they are ready to ascend.

All souls will evolve at some point and all paths will unfold in perfect timing as they are designed to do so. For every being that chooses to open up to the offerings and synchronicities of ascension, the path will be clear. Ascension still requires action, intent, and aligning with the constantly changing energetic blanket upon Gaia. All will unfold in perfect timing and in perfect design.

Power to Choose

We are the primary creators of all events and circumstances that we experience, and therefore we can choose to feel helpless and worthless and take on the energy of the victim, or we can choose to let all situations and events serve us in some expansive way. Our creation potential really is unlimited and infinite and this level of integration in every situation you create will allow you to sense your own mastery within this glorious manifestation experience.

Is there a sense of knowingness within you that is unshakable? Regardless of how challenging or overwhelming an event may appear, if you approach all events with the energy, intent, excitement, and anticipation for a harmonious outcome, then you powerfully shift the events that unfold. Knowingness creates, and it is a powerful vibration and in alignment, that creates surety. If you know a thing to be true, so it shall be. This is the essence of knowingness in which a master walks. You have the power to create all of this from within, and create the peace, love, and harmony you desire.

If we approach what is occurring in our world with a positive energy, we can alter the world and the systems within it so that they serve all of humanity. Although it is important to understand that some events just need to play out to enable the learning of lessons associated with those events. This does not mean that we should sit back and do nothing. It means that we can let go of judgement, hate, and fighting the fight for the sake of fighting. These are old energies of a three dimensional reality and old human behaviours; behaviours that vibrate in negativity and override our desires to create and choose peace.

The power to choose is to choose the vibration that will create a state of awareness of the reality that we wish to inhabit. You will create the vision of an Earth full of harmony, peace, and allowance of spirit. If this is the essence to which you set yourself to vibrate within, we will position ourselves to exude a vibration of love, light, and human potential in order to influence the vibration that is causing all the global issues. You can make a difference by setting your core vibration to a state of balance, harmony, love, light, and unconditional compassion, then the reality you perceive will adjust to make it so, not just for you, but also for everyone and everything around you. The stronger you become, the more you will influence your surroundings, and the greater your influence will spread.

These aspects of understanding Universal energy are key, and even though the masses may not believe what they cannot see, know that all you need to do is focus your attention on your personal alignment and your inner work. *As within, so without.*

Beliefs and Fears

The fears of our forebears have resulted in a belief system that has strengthened the power of the veil to bind us to ignorance and darkness. Even when our subconscious whispers to us of great transcendence, our beliefs encourage us to dismiss it as imagination.

Some ancient masters chose to forge ahead regardless, and there are countless stories of such individuals suffering for their lack of conformity. Some lost their lives, others were cast out, but some managed to share their enlightenment journeys and today we can enjoy their inspiring stories of awakening and ascension. They gave us so much when they threw off the fear derived social controls that limited their (and our) potential for freedom from fear and spiritual poverty.

Beliefs

It is essential to redefine what we believe to be true by reflecting on our beliefs and fears and releasing those that no longer serve us. In so doing, our reality will shift and unblock the flows of Universal energy, thus enabling us to become masters of creation.

First, we change ourselves and then we change the world, for as our energies change the energies of the planet will shift to follow suit. As we, together with Gaia, align with the Universal flow of energy, we become whole.

Beliefs are the foundation of our experiences and the more

profoundly we believe something, the greater potential it has to manifest into our reality. When a vibration of knowingness resides within us and freely flows through us, we create the circumstances and opportunities that we desire. What we perceive is what we experience. We will be filled with a galactic human intelligence that will enable us to sense our way around all obstacles.

The veil that dropped after the fall of Atlantis was inspired by dark and greedy leaders that led by instilling fear and doubt about who we were as a people. Truths about our innate creative abilities, our sensate skills to rise above, have all been skillfully kept from us. We have been fed beliefs and notions and few have challenged them. We have been conditioned to believe lies that keep so many powerless and poor in order for those in power to maintain their power, even if so many suffer because of it.

Enough people have awakened that the belief that we are only deserving of the essentials, mediocre living conditions, and limited financial security is being rejected at all levels of society. Limitation, famine, war, greed, and control reside in old 3rd dimensional frequency, and as we ascend up, we leave behind these struggles and injustices to create a better way of living.

As we redesign our belief systems, our perceptions and state of knowingness will also realign, and our potential will synchronistically expand in alignment with our newfound beliefs. This is how reality is created all around us. We create every aspect of our reality, so now that we know this, we align with what provides us with excitement, ecstasy, bliss, joy, abundance, and whatever else we decide to experience. Being aware of, and entangling with, all that surrounds us can enable greater expansion, potential, meaning, and intimacy so that we naturally unleash our true natural Divine spirit essence.

From these newfound beliefs and self-recognitions, we will build our collective confidence and awareness to act on socio-political issues out of inspiration rather than desperation. For again, awareness and ascension require change, and creating change requires us to get honest about what is, and shift to the vibration of what can be. Whether we can see the potential or possibility does not matter. What matters to the manifestation process is that we know it is possible. The intention to live an inspired and awakened life requires that we not only think but also act in the direction of what we desire. True change requires that we first 'be' the vibration and the energetic alignment of what we wish to experience, and thus our environment mirrors this new frequency.

As we experience and hear about lightship or UFO sightings and incidences similar to that of the Roswell UFO Incident of 1947, or the Phoenix Lights Incident of March 1997, we are given the opportunity to confront our feelings, our beliefs, and our fears about these experiences.

There are no accidents. These experiences float into our reality and when they do, they give us the opportunity to seek within and determine what our beliefs truly are. What do we believe to be true about who we are, where we have been seeded from, what is our purpose and place within the cosmos, and what fears we own and why about the potential for future contact and human evolution?

If we are not reflecting and asking the questions that can allow for honest and respectful insight, then we are missing out on opportunities to expand and create the potentials for profound human evolution.

Perceptions are molded from our belief systems, our

heritage and upbringing, and educational and societal influences. All that we perceive is taken right from the level of awareness we carry. If we desire to expand what we are aware of, the perceptions follow suit. If we have been fed, conditioned, or held limiting beliefs over a vast period of time, with little variation or opportunity for expanded thought, then we may remain somewhat stagnant in our evolutionary process.

Fear

In addition to reflecting on the fears that limit us in this lifetime, it is also important to meditate and discover the fears that left a mark on our souls in past lives. These psychic remembrances can be just as limiting and the archaic beliefs that have been passed from one generation to the next. In awakening, we can heal the wounds of any tragic lifetimes, miseries, imbalances, and limiting belief structures and as we heal, the veil will fall away.

Without the veil to restrict us, we can employ magical systems based on love, fairness, abundance, compassion, and light for all peoples. We will create and manifest all we desire.

Fear is the catalyst for our habitual spending habits, social maladies, and the lack of awareness within our collective. The maturity of our collective consciousness has not been at the level where changes in these systems could occur.

But, that is changing. Inspired people are gathering from all corners of our planet and creating enlightened platforms and portals for higher thought, which is inspiring workable solutions for the many problems that ail our social systems. The people are creating social change and not relying on governments to bring about the change to make our world a better place.

So many now desire a healthier planet, healthier food, honest governments, as well as financial and medical systems that serve all people and are stepping forward to say, "enough is enough!" The time is now to create our higher vibrating Earth. The process of ascension provides us the ability to not only create a better world, but to open communications with higher beings that can assist us along every step of this path. There is great work to be done.

It is important to take courage and be brave, even as we are subjected to incidences of chaos as the old energy takes its last gasping breaths. Focus on the light, follow your excitement, and do not be drawn in by the drama, fear, and doubts that cling to this chaotic backlash.

Three Dimensional Vibrations

The raising of our individual and collective consciousness is an integrative process and integration is crucial for any process of evolution and expansion. Planetary ascension is an energetic shifting on a much larger scale. Gaia is shifting, altering her core resonance, and integrating the higher streams that are being sent and absorbed from every level. This incremental process allows us to receive, absorb, process, and integrate new refined streams and packets of energetic and cosmic information. As we shift the consciousness paradigm of humanity from being one struggling for survival to one glowing with love and unlimited potential, we are shedding the three dimensional vibrations that restrict our consciousness.

As we expand into our new heightened state, our energetic states require more, indeed, we crave more. Ascension is not only the process of opportunity given to each human being to expand in a more enlightened and positive way, it is to also bring our planet, the galaxy, and the cosmos into higher spiritual alignment to heightened states of Oneness through our expanding awareness.

Nothing is left out of the ascension process and as we are mirrors of the same One Source essence, we truly are all One. Everything in Creation is a recipient of every moment. Contact is not only to know more about our cosmos, but it will allow us to know more about who we are within the greater whole, and shedding the 3rd dimensional fears and limitations will allow us to take that next step upon the evolutionary path that has been designed by Source.

You have always had this power and it takes conscious awareness to shed what no longer fits, and as we let go of the excuses, fear, limitation, and the vibration of victimization, we gain greater strength and ability to take hold of what is, in this now moment.

As we expand our awareness to create infinite potential, the infinite ability to choose, we energetically join. The vibration of the collective is shifting and rising in its light quotient with every shift that one person creates. In each procession of expansion, we create the change that allows us to act in a unified, loving, unconditional, and compassionate way.

We are seeing the beginning stages of an illuminated human species, where the goodness and light within, the desire to live and act with compassion, altruism, and love are our guiding principles as we create the systems to energetically match this profound vibration. This is the essence of an ascending planet. It is what is required for us to slip into the cradle of the Universal kingdom of light.

As a collective, we are opening ourselves to expanded learning with each step forward in the way of light. We become free to explore and free to express the multi-dimensional brilliance in which we were created to experience. This is how the mere act to unveil your authenticity can create every step on your ascension path, and in turn offers the vibration for others to do the same.

As I reflect upon the state of being that I was resonating at only eight years ago, I realize that it was much different from the vibration at which I resonate now. This path of awakening has revealed aspects of myself that I had no idea existed. Not only have I manifested synchronicity beyond belief, but also I've regained personal awareness, higher levels of consciousness, intimate reconnection with spirit, and the ongoing remembrance of the mystery and magical essence that Gaia and the Universe offers. All of these beautiful discoveries have brought about the most amazing experiences that can only be described as life altering and profound.

Resistance

There are roughly seven billion people on Earth, and all are vibrating at various frequencies based on their beliefs, conditionings, and understandings. Global ascension will occur when everyone's frequency aligns with the higher frequencies of a 5th dimensional existence, but the process of bringing everyone into alignment is an intricate process that requires planning, skill, grace, and utter benevolence for the safety and greater good of all beings taken into account.

We are all infinite beings of light and we all have freewill to choose a path that feels most appropriate for our level of understanding in that moment. And let's be honest, discussions of Universal energy and ascension is still too heady and esoteric to be fully understood by most people even though it is happening to all of us right here and right now.

Triggers for awakening and rates of ascension are unique to each person and due to the prevalence of limiting histories and teachings; there is a propensity to resist those prompts to tune in to the profound changes occurring all around us. And there are those who will actively work toward creating chaos in an attempt to derail the ascension process. They will not succeed.

Our quickening path is aligning us, dear lighted ones, and we will always have the freewill to go along for the ride, or sit it out. One does not have to study or be involved in the metaphysical field, or take classes in esoteric teachings to come along for this ride. We live within a benevolent Universe and the benevolence pours forth from every being and species that assists the Divine in this ascension for Gaia. One merely has to intend, with purity of heart, to explore ascension and the accelerating path. There is an excitement within that has never been felt, there are whispers from the soul, and there are increasing desires for life to flow with harmony and peace.

Chapter VI

Reprogramming

Choose to Reprogram

The ultimate power of humanity is to rise above any limitation and to choose anything we desire to experience. The question is, how can we create an inspiring environment to support, encourage, and inspire our spiritual expansion and growth?

Knowingness taps you into a level much more profound than mere belief. Self-clarity and knowingness are the most profound tools in the manifestation and transformation process. Trusting who you are right now allows whatever you energetically create to unfold with fluidity and profundity.

Our level of knowingness is directly related to what we experience in our life. What we know will also allow us to intuitively choose what feels right within our ever-expanding potential because as we shed old limitations and escape fear and feelings of limited self-worth. Right here, right now, what do you know to be true about who you are and what do you desire from the world?

If we take ownership and action for creating love, tolerance, and compassion in our everyday lives, we can then experience the result that these powerful emanations create. The more tuned in we are to what we are truly entangled with and what potential we carry, the grander experience we manifest because we intend it so. This is how ascension and evolution works. When we are stirred and shaken to the point that sitting back is no longer an option, we seek, we act, and we create the shifts required to dig ourselves out of what is no longer serving us. We simply must act.

As we take action with pure intent and the purity within our hearts, we automatically move in the direction of a more loving and healthy, and balanced society. We begin to create a society that serves the collective, and the greater good of all beings will be our driving intent because we have expanded our awareness to know we are an aspect of the All.

We have come so far, dear lighted ones, and to idly sit by and do nothing would simply not be an option for those of us that desire change, intimacy, love, and Universal Unity. We have existed on this gorgeous planet for so long, and even with many misconceptions, corruptions, devastations, and mistruths about who we are and why we are here, we still have the profound power within to shift it all within this now moment. To awaken into a new energetic paradigm that will transform who we are, as a human species requires that we first seek higher resolve and answer the call within. All aspects and attributes that make up this human experience can merge once again into a state of balance, harmony, unconditional love, and Oneness with All That Is. You are capable of manifesting this multi-dimensional brilliance.

Refining Our Vibration

It is imperative that we bring all our fears, limitations, and negative beliefs to the surface so that each can be transformed so that we can be transformed. We cannot change what we do not own and we cannot connect or see the new revelations awaiting us on the path to ascension if our vibrations and frequencies are restricted by the darkness of fear and despair.

As we address each negative frequency, we shed layers of

restriction and our sensitivity to energy frequencies increases, allowing us to imbue the essence of all the wonderful things that match our new frequency. Our sensitivity will increase as we become more entangled, thus making further entanglement easier. We adjust and refine at every stage.

These adjustments include the progressive changing of beliefs, definitions, and behaviours that surface in our alignment work to adjust to divinely sent frequencies. Failing to adjust will result in a gap between what is coming in and what we can handle and the challenge to our physical bodies can be overwhelming. There will be kick back and resistance if the old residues are not cleared. Even if you don't notice it, see it, or acknowledge it, we are energetic beings of light and we are constantly sending and receiving energy. It is our responsibility to engage our innate skills to ensure we are in tune with the Universe. It is important to continually work with our beliefs in order to move and navigate through this vibrational tunnel.

Once we begin the process of refining our environment, we will find that we are more effective at maintaining homeostatic balance and harmony with our environment.

As our environment is altered, we will need to adjust, alter, and refine our whole being in order to maintain our progress in ascension. Feelings of being unloved, a sense of lack, or even feeling out of control will affect our progress. Thankfully, when such negative vibrations exist, they force the associated issues to the surface so that we can address them. Once we are on the path of ascension, anything that pushes us out of alignment will be glaringly obvious making this process a foolproof mechanism. Pretending or suppressing what is there will only prolong the challenge and friction between the conflicting frequencies and will result in an escalation of manifestations in our reality until we address and clear the issues.

The energies that assist this planetary ascension come from many different levels. We have planetary grids that align with other celestial and galactic anchors. Our sun and moon, as well as all of the astrological alignments, play a part in the energetic refinement and amplification for Gaia. There are also many different cosmic groups, and councils of beings that are so deeply connected and in love with humanity that they commit their lifetime to serving us. Some beings act as spirit guides, some act as communicators in the process, some beings act as energetic amplifiers, and on and on. Just as other beings are entangled with Gaia and humanity in this grand Universal Source plan for ascension, we too become entangled with these beings. Along with these many outside sources of energetic worker helping Gaia and humanity, there is the work we do as active participants in this ascension party. This goes to prove that there is nothing that is left out of the process of ascension and there is always an opportunity for every being to take part in the ascending energies occurring right now on this planet.

The process of following our individual paths with excitement will result in a greater understanding and more opportunities to recreate ourselves. Each day is a new opportunity to redefine our paths and steer ourselves in powerful new directions. The expansion that we are allowing for ourselves will ultimately bring all of humanity to an illuminated state with every vibrational increment that we as individuals align with. We will be Illuminated Galactic Humans, as we literally aligning our vibrational states to a point where we glow — just as the many light beings that are assisting us in our expansion glow.

The Power of Words

Ascension and expansion are very powerful words and have the ability to create a sense of remembrance. If you sit and merely ruminate on these words, you will expand within these thoughts alone. These words invite you into bigger realms, wider skies, and deeper insights. We have been conditioned to create meanings for words so that we can navigate our way through this physical reality. One cannot think about the words *ascension* and *expansion* without coming up with a picture and definition of growth or change.

When these words are spoken, something within us activates and we will feel the urge to find how these words fit within us and how we will move around them as we process their meaning. There are certain words that are encoded with profound Source essence. Words activate energetic memories and movement, at the DNA level, galactic level, Source level, and at our spirit level. We will be spurred into action to seek a grander understanding. Words allow us to remember who we are at the soul level and allow us to explore and seek the higher meaning and understandings of our full expansiveness. The language we use is steeped in vibratory resonance that can trigger us to reflect, feel or react in a deeper way in knowingness that we are more than we thought. Our language and our definitions and beliefs are all aspects we can refine so our experience can be altered.

There are certain words that create a reaction so powerful that we are able to scan our multi-dimensional memory to recall what we know about them. When we take a thought or an idea and create the definitions, we integrate further what this thought may mean in our life. Our brains automatically start to process information and then compartmentalize it into various segments so that our physical mind can understand and file it where it best fits based on our beliefs and conditioning at the time.

Let us take the word *contact*, for example. As we read this word, it will trigger feelings, emotions, ideas, senses, and so on. We then allow the word to sink in deeper, as our brain automatically files it to the best-fit scenario within us. If we have been fed information of fear and uncertainty about this word, we react in accordance to those conditions. We are influenced by society, family, and education centres. We can see, in this one example, how one word can conjure unparalleled denseness and we have not even discussed its profound potential upon our lives. The words we use can be twisted and cause reactions that shut down the potential for enlightenment and expansion.

Let us move through the process of understanding this word *contact.* Contact can mean many things based on where we are intellectually, spiritually, and emotionally. When hearing this word a few years ago, I was intrigued and excited to understand why I felt such excitement. I soon found myself synchronistically gifted with books on the subject. Channelled material flowed to me anytime I had the television on. I began to see deeper connections to the synchronicities that would occur and I looked further into all that was energetically gifted to me. Synchronicities are like a fun, energetic puzzle that my guides would offer to allow me to dig deeper and seek within for the reason behind my intrigue.

Words have a way of showing us something we need to see and if there are certain words, phrases, pictures, or sounds that stand out, then reflect upon them and ask for guidance.

In my process of self-reflection, meditation, and honing my

Divine skills, I recognize that inner tug as a message that something profound is waiting for me on the path and to keep a look out. The insistent whispers or intuitive feelings about topics, words, courses, or even books are the soul's way of directing our path to an expanded understanding.

There have been countless times when I felt a swirling sensation within my gut or a thought that kept coming to the forefront of my mind, or even images in my dreams. My guides or my Higher Self's were telling me, "Think about this."

Ascension, for me, first came from the internal pulling, hinting, tugging, and guidance from our Higher Self. Afterwards, I take what is found in my reality and merge all that I have learned and reflected upon what it means to me in this now moment. This is how the effort, the seeking, and the understanding we choose to move through life is directly related to our expansion and ascension. It is a process of expanding on who we were a moment before and then grounding our newfound beliefs with action. Ascension and expansion can begin as we bring topics that stir something within to the forefront, for deeper understanding and realignment to what fits our ever-changing world and the frequency we desire.

Universal Unity

Universal unity is not an easy concept to master. The inner path-work and self-reflection required to create Oneness entails letting go of lifetimes of judgement, fear, distaste, and misunderstandings of not only other humans, but also for all those beings off our planet. This is the work of the masters.

Ascension requires the integration of new ideas and beliefs that brings you to a heightened perspective. Through heightened awareness, we gain greater self-love and self-respect, and what we gain for ourselves seeps into everything we experience. Perspective and belief is the cornerstone of how we experience life, and therefore, once we work through our belief systems, and how we define things, then what we perceive in our reality shifts.

Sometimes these shifts are profound, and sometimes they are barely noticeable. Whatever level or increment the shift may be though, all of it is required in planetary ascension. Each new thought of positive light, heightened feelings of compassion, and loving disposition sets the ripple on the pond of our planet and triggers other changes within our collective consciousness. Not only does this ripple of light affect our planet and all life upon it, the love and light you emit is also woven throughout Creation. This is what is meant by, "We are all One." Every change, shift, and alteration in belief, changes the whole.

As we are bombarded with warring drama that's played out in several pockets around the world, we're sometimes tested to dig deep and create positive light from what we see. These stories that are playing out are the jostling effect between old belief systems and new Earth frequency, and it is the friction of these two opposing energies that creates the abrupt reactions and negative and drama that we see. We can do a great deal of good in the world by centring ourselves and sending loving thoughts, peaceful thoughts, and harmonious frequencies to war-torn regions of the Earth.

Universal Unity is the concept about finding the commonality in all beings, and knowing at the core of who we are within Creation, that we are One. The power of only a few positive people is enough to shift an entire army, so never underestimate the power of light and love, for it is the vibration of Creation.

If it is our desire to open up to the process of ascension, then we are faced with the inner work that must be brought to light as we prepare ourselves for imminent contact, first landings, and reintegration with our interstellar families. We were not meant to be stagnant and floating alone in space for an eternity. For aeons now, we have been lovingly supported, guided, and blessed from afar, and our planet, our frequency, and our cosmos has been and is being prepared for the imminent shift to a 5th dimensional home. In these profound energetic shifts, we must understand that to have this immense ascension complete, there needs to be a unification of countless beings spanning the Universe committed to Gaia's transition. Some of these beings are the family members, the celestial teams that have assisted us in traumatic events, and even watched over us as our spirit guides.

If change, greater entanglement, and intimacy with life is what you truly desire, then seek out the books, groups, and events that allow you to dream in like vibrations, for if it inspires and stirs you from within, there is a link that you own and it may be timely to discover what that link is.

Every expanded action you act upon expands the All, and the vibration of that action goes directly into the grids and the overall potential of our new Earth. Universal energy touches us all in an infinity motion, ensuring that all aspects of Creation is touched by the benevolence of Source residing at the centre of our Universe. Allow yourself to muse on concepts of Source, Universal love, Universal Unity, expansion, deeper thought, reflection, and consideration, for every thought leads to another and blooms into new heightened beliefs that serve you in powerful ways.

To honour these concepts in the light that is deserved, we must ask ourselves about the beliefs we hold about those in our neighbourhood or even in our own homes, and how we can heal and honour these relationships. Universal unity begins at home in the moment of now, for everything within your immediate experience is a reflection of what is going on within, right now. How can we really offer kinship to another species when we are fighting with grave misunderstandings and judgements about societies within our worldly family? This is a powerful question and requires us to dig deep within and answer honestly, so that we can unify all that we are immersed within. We must allow honesty and compassion to guide us as we move beyond where we are and expand to a heightened potential of what we can be. You cannot change what you do not own, and to live in the essence of true Divine Oneness and unity with all beings and species means that we must look at our deepest, darkest places and heal what needs to be healed. Acceptance, respect, and oneness can then be achieved for a glowing new Earth potential.

Expanding Consciousness

Consciousness is awareness, and awareness is consciousness. What allows individual and even planetary consciousness to expand and offer access to an energetic portal than permits growth is the acceptance of the idea that there may be more to existence than we ever thought.

We are mirrors of our planet, and the planet is the mirror of what we resonate. We are all a reflection of one another. We are all entangled within this quantum cosmic web of Creation as as we search for truth we are opening ourselves and our planet up inspiration and awareness of the secrets of Creation that have been encoded within our cells and our consciousness. As our consciousness expands, each layer of the multi-verse is affected as well. With every single change, there is the change within the whole. For every thought, word, and act that you choose to emit goes into Creation with your specific energetic imprint upon it.

The consciousness that is you, beyond this illusory physical body, is your catalyst to experience anything, and as you attune yourself with its desire to expand and explore, you can move to a heightened frequency or manifest anything you desire. Like a beautiful immense quilt with an infinite number of patterns, threads, designs, and textures, so too are we in the blanket of Creation, and if one thread or one stitch was missing, the quilt would not be complete. The potential of expansion is what we see humanity evolving to with a planet glowing in loving support of it. We truly are the catalyst to achieving transformation on this planet, and we are being inspired into action by the potential that peaks beyond the horizon.

Chapter VIII

Tools

We have been gifted with and blessed with many tools to enable our ascension. Tools such as freewill, creativity, imagination, our physical bodies, and many innate gifts encoded within our very cells. The most infinitely profound tool that we have access to is our consciousness. There is no app, and there is no android or tablet that can come close to what we can create with this amazing gift with its capacity to expand and evolve and enable us to create and recreate who and what we are as well as the world around us.

We have been gifted with incredible tools that will allow us to align ourselves with the multi-dimensional reality in which we exist. We own physical tools, energetic tools, innate tools and all are Divinely encoded to support and honour each other in this incredible process we call life. As we begin to better understand these tools and create the entanglement that we were designed to do, we will free the potential that humanity truly has.

These tools will enable us to sense higher forms of energy, to receive celestial messages, to create eco-friendly systems that will sustain and serve our planet, or even to create the landing pad for first contact with highly evolved beings and our celestial family members.

Time and Space

Each realm of existence offers specific rules and tools to assist us as we create our experiences. As we learn to understand the rules and tools of our spirit essence, we will be better able to move with greater fluidity and let go of the structure, rigidity, and limitations of our physical incarnation.

Of particular interest is the illusory nature of time. As we let go of our need to control a linear mindset, we will be able to float quite naturally into a multi-dimensional mindset that allows us to experience, or at least energetically sense any time line. All of the experiences we have ever lived are in fact occurring right now and we actually have the ability to tap into any time line, if we so choose. We can experience the essence of travelling inter-dimensionally, or shifting from one reality to another instantaneously, if it serves us to do so. Our Higher Self offers up these types of experiences to enable us gain perspective on how our vibrations affect our experiences. The more we understand our reality, the here and the now, and the laws that govern it, the more adept we can become at letting go of the ones that no longer serve us.

In awakening, we learn to align, trust, allow, and open in the now, to create the vibration that allows us to shift to the information we need to serve us in this now, regardless of where or when that information manifests. Of course, such an ability is not automatic, as one must necessarily complete certain levels of inner work, commitment, and reverence before it will be possible to unleash these profound potentials. It is essential that one resonate at a vibration of benevolence before one can access such energetic activations.

The Universal laws cannot be circumvented as they are only for the serving of the greater good and as Source sees fit. To live in loving communion with our world, one another, and all within existence are the primary attributes of any secret knowledge, and to create our own unique expression under these laws in a respectful, loving, and benevolent way is always held in the highest of regard first.

We have all agreed, during our time at a higher level of our existence, that time and space is a tool that can allow us a unique perspective of this physical reality. It is also a wonderful lesson when we can finally let these constructs go in during our ascension process. On this physical plane, we have chosen time and space as a factor or a tool in our manifestation process. Once we fully understand time and space, we can then redefine it and even let go of its limitations.

As we let go of this time-space constraint, we will begin to feel our lives shift in both subtle and profound ways. We will begin to sense life moving through us in a variety of ways and we can then expand our consciousness enough to experience our other multi-dimensional selves, our inter-galactic connections and family, and we will start to experience instant manifestation — if we so desire. We will touch on the value of our ability to 'let go' of limiting beliefs as we move through this material so that you can, in turn, do the same in your own life with your own beliefs and definitions.

Time and space are constructs used in this realm. As we expand our awareness, our understanding of time will change and we will experience more and more unexplainable situations where time can appear to go missing or appear to stop,. Sometimes we may even experience the sensation of moving through something faster than we thought could be possible. Time is essentially collapsing and will continue to do so until we shift into the 5th dimension.

This shift in our perception of time and space is an attribute of ascension and will be seen and felt by many people. The rush of refined patterns swirling through our consciousness can no longer be denied. The resonance will be palpable and it is so very exciting.

Whether the multi-dimensional experiences or visitations occur in a meditation or dreamtime, know that we have more ability to shift time and space than we know. So the next time you feel as if time is slipping away, celebrate, and fall into these moments for the vibration you are setting is truly accelerating.

The Internet

The Internet has offered any person from any location the ability to seek in ways that no other piece of technology has done. It has become a great tool that allows people from every corner of the world to connect with others in a like-vibrational manner and together create greater light. It has enabled the creation dialogue and pathways for others to tap into and platforms that bring us together in unity so that we can collaborate to emit our profound desires for freedom, creative expression, and truth about our human potential.

The Internet has truly opened up opportunities for us to explore our potential. It is the portal through which we can take action, to discover, create, and support the process of redefining the life we choose to live and experience. In our most expanded state, in the future years of new Earth, the physical connection that the Internet facilitates will be replaced by an ability to link telepathically with all other beings, and resonate at our highest consciousness state in a natural and ascended way. Just as the other ascended planets have evolved to, we too will have our day of peace, harmony, magical transformation, and unlimited potential.

We are letting go of all that we used to know, and we are stepping up into the unknown, for even the unknown has to be better the drama playing out before us over the past four thousand years. There have long been pockets of spiritual mavericks persevering with unquestionable faith, for the potential that we know resides within for us. This is one path that we can design in our own unique way and the Internet has opened the door for those who seek enlightened portals of potential to immerse themselves in a vibration that finally feels like it fits. With each new phase of ascension, we are literally creating new energetic potentials. Within these potentials sit higher resonating experiences, and like a wave that expands and grows, awakening is the wave that is gaining profound momentum.

Trust

When we are in a state of trust, we not only honour that of what resides around us, but we have a deep seeded trust in who we are and what we desire to create for ourselves. Trust allows us to know that we are profound beings of Divine light essence and all that we manifest will serve us in some way. Aligning all that unfolds to you with positive vibrations will ensure a positive experience will be set.

If we are in a state of constant worry, questioning, or fear or if we react with anger or impatience, then we are telling the Universe, "I do not trust myself to manifest greatness. I do not trust what is coming to me. I am not worthy of manifesting." Negative dialogue, self-talk, fear, doubt, and worry can only manifest a life that aligns with the lower vibrations associated with these characteristics.

Trusting Creation, Source, and all of life is powerful. To know with certainty, to create the unwavering faith of the Masters will allow us to manifest a profoundly purposeful life. We will see the magic in all that unfolds and in all that is created.

I have used the vibration of surrender many times with my own personal manifestation and ascension path, for one of my life themes is to release all deep seeded trust issues and fully awaken into benevolence of this profound experience. Surrender allows us to release all worry, fear, and doubt and simply move with the flow of Universal brilliance. We will always be protected, loved, and supported as we follow the highest vibrations because this is how the Universe operates.

Trust your ability to create brilliance, trust what flows forth from the Universe, Source, and Creation and know all can serve if we so define and design it to. We have this power.

If trust and love imbue our dominant vibrations, then our life experience will only mirror this back to us.

Operating from an allowing state of mind is a vibrational match to the concept of expansion and ascension, for we know that ascension is integrative. We allow all to unfold and integrate because we know it holds value, honour, and respect in the eyes of Source. Trust, allowance, and surrender is held within the vibration of knowingness and when you bring all that you know to resonate with these powerful levels of knowingness, there is nothing you cannot experience or manifest. These are the vibrations that flow with 'pulsar-like' power throughout the cosmos. If we live with this level of freedom, trust, and love toward one another, we begin to set the stage for the inevitable contact with beings from off our world.

Trust in the blueprint you designed, and trust in such Universal laws. Ascension allows us the acceptance, love, and understanding that we all deserve the same freedom and respect to follow our own paths, for we are all uniquely created in this way.

Love

When love is activated within, there is nothing that will stand in your way of knowing, experiencing, and being more of it. Love creates light, and it truly is the most powerful vibration in Creation, it intrigues, it spawns, it births, it creates, it heals, it empowers, it transforms, it transcends, it is LOVE. We understand that flowing with the wave of light just 'feels' better. Our reality is being stretched and refined in every way to be able to go the distance and support every ascending human.

Until the concepts of Universal energy, ascension, and enlightenment reach mass understanding and acceptance, we still act as individuals to propel our own path in the ways we desire. One cannot wait for others to catch-up. This life is designed for you, by you, and it is only you that can create the light to ignite it in powerful ways. Embrace your innate power to create and align with such refined states of being. We can then go about our lives with greater purpose and clarity, and have understanding and compassion for others to move about their path, for all paths are purposeful and required.

The power of love you have within is truly unlimited and if

we imbue this level of love, in every moment, every experience, we begin to create not only greater balance for ourselves and Gaia, but we further enmesh ourselves within the greater weaving that is All That Is.

We are literally attuning ourselves to manifest a physical experience to expand in all ways that the Universe will offer us. We choose life themes, our blueprint, the purpose, callings, themes, and even those we are surrounded by. We have perfectly planned and designed it all and as we expand to our desired heightened state, the process of this transformation shifts what used to be fear based, dark, and negative, and allows Universal Divine light, Source light to heal and expand. What no longer aligns with our preferred states of being will become so glaringly obvious that we will be shown what requires release or shifting. This is how ascension, love, and light work within our framework and reality.

As we transcend into higher frequencies, all darkness will stand out for attention and transformation, for remember there is no real thing that is dark, there is only the absence of light, the absence of love, the absence of acknowledgement for who we truly are, and understanding for what we have resonated within since our earliest of incarnation.

We are truly profound beings of light, and we have the potential to transcend any challenge, darkness, difficulties, and reengage and reconnect with all life in the most intimate of ways. As a collective, we have lost our way many times, over many centuries, and never before have we been offered the support, love, and balance to recreate something profound with our newly heightened awareness. There is no other tool in Creation that matches the brilliance, power, and vibrational atonement that love offers, and as we refine the innate powers of our consciousness to accept and reverberate with these streams of Source, we redefine humanity and Gaia. So understand dear lighted ones, that darkness is only the absence of love.

Light created from unconditional love is the highest energetic alignment that one can seek. We are patterns of light; all things in the Universe are an aspect of energy, and energy is light. Aligning oneself with the highest of vibrations is the key in staying abreast on the wave of light that will carry us into an ascended Earth experience. Don't give in to what you are being sold or told. Know that any war, any fight, and any combat is always fought with those who have access to the deepest of pockets and who desire to fight fire with fire. Just as you have choice and freewill, so too does every other human. Choose love in all that you do.

Love is the most powerful element and vibration within our Universe and you will shift the resonance in all you perceive if you act out of the purity of love.

The masters have eschewed aggression because they know in their deepest spirit essence that love conquers all. Love will always align us with our highest and best interests. If you create and send loving tweets, or loving, light-filled blogs in order to express a spirit essence of purity, integrity, and love you will align with the Divine. If you choose to define, act, and behave in loving and peaceful ways, so too will your reality align with you in all that you manifest. Imagine and perceive a brighter humanity. Visualize yourself being on and living within the new Earth reality. Any positive and loving imagery will assist in creating heightened vibrations for new Earth potentials. So stand in love for humanity. As many of the great masters and wise seers have stated, *If you fight fire, with fire, you will only get more fire.* You cannot solve any issue from the same state of energy in which the issue resides. We must rise above and create a higher alignment from within to create the wisdom in which global answers will be found.

We are immensely complex and uniquely expansive energetic beings, always changing and evolving with each new thought. It is no accident that our heart is the most powerful device that allows us the ability to not only connect with others in our multi-verse, but open to our own infinite power to commune with our Divine essence. With every heartbeat, we automatically send out ripples of energetic communication with our own unique signature pattern of personal energetic pulses; vibratory messages that pierce with lightning speed into the Universal ethers. Science and medicine will soon confirm the speculation that we are much more profound than the physical encasement that we have allowed ourselves to be fixed within for centuries.

We are multi-dimensional and multi-faceted, and just as our thoughts and beliefs are very real in their power to create and manifest, so too is the innate energetic imprint that lies within every living being. The level of connection we have with our whole aspect can be sent and initiated at the heart level and is the essence of manifestation. The heart is the Universal tool that links us to All That Is, and it is the primary tool in conjunction with our ability to expand and ascend, for all experience is heart-based.

You can practice using heart-centred techniques and other heart projected emotions for higher loving, healing, and more honest and intimate communication for all. Visualize your heart energetically linking with the heart of those that you entangle with every day, and you will see the results of this heart connection transform your situations and events. Messages of loving and compassionate intent can have profound effects on the entire world that ripple through the Universe and span the globe, even if we start within the home. This is the concept behind distance healing and other telepathic communications. Telepathy, distant healing, and even manifestation can propel into the ethers with emotional integrity and the purity of intent that we hold at the heart level. If we open every aspect of our lives and initiate intent through the heart, there is no limit to what we are able to achieve and transform.

When we create our communication and manifestations from the heart level, we are creating the alignment that's in the highest and best for the soul. The power we place into an intent that resides at the heart level, is profoundly more powerful than that of wishful thinking or goal setting. As we amp-up our own personal vibrations, we become more attuned with other beings that resonate within the same or at least similar 'stations' as we do. This type of heart-based connection allows the intuitive energetic flow of information to remain open and benevolent. Creating from our heart base is always positive, loving, and can create the most powerful intentions with light and healing vibrations by centring our emotions, grounding the Divine essence within, and sending it out to the Universe with profundity and purpose to be returned in synchronistic and magical ways.

Gratitude and Appreciation

Gratitude and appreciation is the fuel that propels all energetic beauty that electrifies our lives. It is an angelic vibration that will align you with all is good and positive. Gratitude and appreciation is the follow-through to all that is being gifted your way and allows the Universe to sense your engagement in this energetic dance.

Gratitude can be expressed in an infinite number of ways. In my daily life, I write, acknowledge, and personally journal the Divine synchronicity that I receive in my life. I acknowledge and embrace each synchronistic act into my being. I integrate the lessons and gifts that each symbolic synchronistic act can teach and in the moment it is received, I send immediate gratitude and appreciation for the level of orchestration it took to be experienced at this physical level.

The myriad of beings that are entangled with our everyday life to awaken and stir us into action are mind-boggling. Gratitude is the language and essence of the Divine and it is a vibration known throughout Creation, just as love and compassion are. When you taste the level of interaction for one encounter to be gifted to you, it truly can bring you to your knees, so be grateful in every day. All that unfolds is the spiritual proof that we are profound beings of light with infinite creator potential

Reverence and gratitude for all that you experience, as well as the detail, the orchestration, and the precision to enable us to align to a new frequency of Universal energy are the attributes and vibrations that will ensure you remain intimately linked with All That Is and all these the magical processes. At any level of existence, gratitude, surrender, and reverence are the vibrations that accelerate any manifestation that you desire to experience. Gratitude is the attitude of all higher frequency realms and is understood at the heart level by all beings within our diverse and brilliant Universe. It is Divine in its nature.

Imagination

We have been blessed with very powerful tools as sensate beings within Creation. Not least among these blessings are freewill and imagination. With these tools, there is nothing that one cannot experience or create. Allowing our imaginations to soar, to play, to tickle our senses in every way possible, is to expand our consciousness. Everything you imagine is achievable. Every wonderful fantasy exists somewhere.

Creation provides us with a playground of infinite energy, bound only by our imagination, so be free, play like a curious child, and explore the magic beyond the infinite portal of possibilities. And as we intend with a purity of heart and with expressions of love in all ways the process of manifesting will become fluid and carefree.

The more we allow ourselves to tap into the infinite potential of what is, the more creative and grander the experience will be. Tie in a state of knowingness with this state of creative consciousness and before we know it we have slipped into a state of allowance for all that unfolds.

This is how the energetic play of all the Universal laws can be expansive in the most powerful of ways. As we release our limited beliefs, as we redefine who and what we are, and as we open up the portal of Divine communication between our Higher Selves, our spirit guides, and celestial teams, we can then playfully ignite the ethers for even greater manifestations. We can link the pull of what we know to be true with the vigour of a passionate and pure heart, knowing there is nothing that we cannot experience or manifest.

Celestial Communication

We can use these techniques to practice and hone these energetic activities for expanding heart to heart communications not only with one another, but with our celestial family. The greater understanding we have to our multi-dimensional aspects, the greater potential we can manifest to create future 5th dimensional socio-economic systems and communication with our celestial neighbours.

Preparing for contact is unique and requires that we allow ourselves to open to the potential that we have not allowed ourselves to tap into before. Instead of following the same pattern of understanding that we have for hundreds of years, in our belief about how to communicate with our celestial family, we can rise up and tune into how it is actually done. I can tell you right now, it does not require spending billions of dollars on telecommunication technology to do so. How many nations could have been fed with the money we spend on this technology or war machines when the answers have always been within?

When we intentionally act from a loving and open heart, with unconditional respect, in the highest interests of all, we merely need to ask from within, telepathically, and the teams linked with you, will respond in kind. That is it. There is no need for the complexity and unnecessary technology.

We have been communicating with the ethers and celestial beings since the seeding of humanity took place. It has been done in alignment with following our hearts desire for

Oneness, connectedness, and entanglement to expand within the potential that we were created with. There will soon come a time when all of humanity will operate in this way. How effective could this be in the various political and economic arenas and bargaining tables that our society relies upon, if we used heart-centred communication?

Heartfelt messages of love and healing can be sent into any situation even before it occurs, allowing us to literally control the outcomes. Sending powerful and loving intent from your heart can align you with any higher potential and you will be assisted and responded to in perfect timing. Communication between our celestial teams and family is instantaneous. There are no boundaries of time or space and technology is not needed. Higher resonating beings have the ability to materialize, or dematerialize instantly.

The celestials merely show their craft for our benefit, as it is a tool used to assist in our awakening, and can slowly allow us to familiarize ourselves with the concept of other life forms within our cosmos.

Aligning with our heart centre energetically prepares the landscape for anything you desire for the heart is a Divine link and a common thread to which we all share. You can relax in your meditations or reflection time in order to send out heartfelt intentions for heightened communications with your team and tune in to the vibration of allowance and trust, and you will see magic unfold before you.

You can send messages for those whom you desire connection with; for instance, your star family or higher aspects of yourself on other dimensions, and with every beat of your heart, the energetic language that is received instantly creates loving resonance that will be returned in some way. There is no time or space in higher dimensional realms, and as love is felt, as love is sent, it is the most powerful vibration in the Universe and will be responded to in kind.

Heartfelt intent, the purity of loving essence within, can be created in simple ways and yet creates powerful emanations that ripple and reverberate throughout the cosmic canvas. Never underestimate the power of heartfelt, compassionate communication. It is the language that all cultures, all realms, and all species recognize and understand for the chemical and energetic transactions that occur with the purity of love, transcends all. Love will always align you with the Divine streams of light and Source.

Divine Essence Affirmation

I am Divine essence. I am alive and well within this magical Universe and with the purity of my heart; I am creating a new reality with every breath. I am healthy, I am wise, and I am abundant in every way. I express myself with loving unification to all beings from the centre of my heart, I emit pure Divine love, and I know it will be returned to me in kind. I am blessed, I am infinite, I trust the path that I create, and I am a powerful creator of mirrored Divine essence. Together, as One, we connect with heartfelt light, and with the highest love and respect for all species and beings, we unite. I AM THAT I AM.

Those attuned to energetic knowingness will pick up on the powerful vibrations in the Universal web and will seek out similar or matching vibrational states. We then receive matching resonant connections that arise in a myriad of ways; a phone call, a meeting with someone, an email from an outside source, an inspiration, an impression from one of your team, can all have profound consequences to your soul path. You can even sense heartfelt communications when you 'sense' someone is in the room with you when it appears, to be empty.

I will validate this for you now, the room is always full. Humanity's greatest lesson in expansion and transcending limitation is to release the mindset that we must see something to know it exists. We breathe air that we cannot see, we use the electricity within our homes that we cannot see, and if we expand this to conscious beings, we can then manifest wholeness and inclusivity within realms that are truly infinite. There is life and consciousness in everything and you are always surrounded, supported, and loved.

Heightened awareness, new opportunities, and circumstances will seem to arise out of thin air as we are gifted with, what was once impossible, unlimited potential from the Divine once we raise our core frequency. Unlimited potential is a frequency, just as love is, imbalance, or bliss. It is within us to act on the simple joys and excitements that arise, and know that magical events that flow to us are offered in our highest and best, because we have set the dial to ecstasy, anticipation, and profundity.

Preparing for contact with higher realm beings, including

your Higher Self, starts first with the heart, and this process can be enhanced as we centre our intent on benevolence, greater awareness, and following the path that Divinity had designed with you in your life-planning sessions. At the highest level of who you are, you knew your potential and ability for awakening. To open you up for expansion in magical ways was one of the primary reasons that inspired you to incarnate at this time. When we combine heart-centred intent with positive emotions in our thoughts, there is truly nothing that we cannot manifest or transform within this reality.

Creative Expression Exercise

Let's practice a 5th dimensional atonement. Imagine your greatest vision. Any desire you wish to experience — creative, intellectual, health, abundance — it is your choice. Choose one that resonates deeply with you.

Imagine every aspect of that vision and how you fit within it. Add details to your vision. Include colours and sounds to the imagery. Think about how things should look and feel and taste and sound. Add as much detail as you can.

Now, expand upon your vision by adding emotions. Feel

what this experience means to you and to those dear to you. Imbue this vision with the intent of a passionate and loving heart; a heart full of expectation to receive this beauty. Know that you are worthy of it, for you are the master creating it. Now, let it go. Let the vision float up into the ether.

Allow the power of your imagination, your intent, your creativity, the purity of your intent, the knowingness of your mastery skills, and your earthly freewill, to choose the most powerful vision to come together in the ethers and permit it to be sent to you in the most profound and perfect timing. The appropriate signals have been sent out to the Universe, and your spirit guides, the angelic realm, your over-soul family, and the celestial team supporting you will all gather and play their part for the unfolding of this glorious creative endeavour. Feel your connection to the Divine.

Surrender the details of this sincere wish to the Universe and enjoy your moment for moment life with pure knowingness that you will always be supported and brought what is in your highest interest in every situation. If you align yourself to a profound vibration, then only a

147

profound result will manifest. It is Universal law.

This simple process can be practiced with anything you desire to manifest. Go beyond limitation, let go of negative beliefs and preconditioned notions then watch the magic unfold. Know that your infinite potential is coded into your imagination, and your imagination is coded into the Divine essence within.

Imagination is the portal in which we move spirit energy and inspiration. There are an infinite number of works of genius in every arena where the inspiration from spirit has altered the way we look at what is possible for human potential. Any master artist, inventor, scientist, or writer knows that feeling when Divine inspiration strikes. It is unmistakable and profound.

When true inspiration hits, the open flow of energy, information, and wisdom within the Universe is accessible for whatever it is we desire to create. Inspiration is fed through our neural pathways and the moment we tell ourselves, our cells, our multi-dimensional aspects that we know the potential for brilliance, we step up into the vibration of a higher resonating human.

Your Higher Self will then take over and deliver the greatest gifts to you every time. Synchronicities, situations, circumstances, and opportunities will float into your reality as a result of these innate engagements between you and your infinite potential. This is the power of entanglement, trust, surrender, and allowance.

Chapter VII

Guides

You have the power to alter your reality and you have all the tools you need to go beyond what you have ever imagined or dreamed could be possible. It all starts by allowing curiosity, your intuition, and above all, your heart to be your guiding compass, for the one who seeks is the one that will expand. To seek is to know more, understand more, and allow the infinite aspects of Creation to be offered to us in our passion to seek more of who we are and what we exist within.

The one who seeks lets go of limitation and separation for there is awareness that allows one to see we are all One. In seeking we relearn, we remember our wholeness, our Oneness, and our greater link with All That Is, and we are intertwined and enmeshed within it all. Those who resonate with Oneness will experience the Earth that matches that vibration.

When we awaken, we will become aware of a team of higher beings who are ready and eager to assist us on our path to ascension. Our team is comprised of various energetic masters and as we move through our life, our spirit guides, and team will change as we grow and learn.

We are always assigned to gifted and perfect guides, celestial being that will assist us in manifesting our life's desires and achieving our soul blueprint. Timing in this way is always perfectly designed into everyone's life contract, and if something is not manifesting, or unfolding, it is due to the lack of connection that we hold about our potential and our reality.

My guides first manifest through my dreams and remarkable synchronicities that could not be attributed to mere coincidence. The links were enough to propel me into a passionate spiritual investigation about why these coincidences were occurring, what they meant, and why my life was taking such an unusual turn. It was not until much later that I understood that all of these magical coincidences were the skillful work of a myriad of brilliantly benevolent beings that had been with me in every moment of my life. The more passionate I became about my awakening, the more I seemed to experience, and the more I would sense and understand at the energetic multi-dimensional level.

Looking back on my childhood now, I can fully understand all the 'strange' occurrences and know that I was always connected, linked, and entangled with these amazing beings and how many times I was led from self-destruction because of their love for me and the potential I owned. What created such loneliness, discomfort, and confusion was only my inability to understand the Universe and Universal energy.

Universal Teams

There are a myriad of beings that have specific roles in the Divine planning, enhancing, and creation of life within every Universe. All of these teams are driven by and in service to the light and love of the All. Many of these benevolent systems of beings, offer their skill, frequency, and light to the service and expansion of the word of Source essence. Groups, committees, and councils traverse the cosmos and design plans, agendas, and mappings for life within galaxies, and all under the watchful and loving eye of Source. This profoundly powerful link is never broken, and the reverence is always adhered to because they know with every ounce of their beingness, that this spirit essence of Creation lies within us all.

The path of ascension offers many things to many beings, and although we sit in a chair, apparently alone, feel the presence of the infinite number of beings that stand with you, arm in arm and breath by breath. As you read these words, take note of what your physical body is showing you in validation of this statement.

Your body will provide clues to your daily existence with the Divine, and if you truly tune in, you will sense the presence of Creation flowing with you through your daily life. I am constantly brought to my knees each day that I experience the lightships above my home, and the higher frequency beings that remind me that I am an entangled and an integral aspect of it all. Creation, Source, and everything within it is consciousness itself, and our consciousness expanding is what will allow us to experience anything we truly desire. I am always finding new levels of respect and reverence for this opportunity to know more.

Our cosmic family, our cosmic playground and school will be the future of the new Earth and our cosmic guides will show us how to refine and express the new illuminated galactic human in new enlightened ways for a healthy, harmonious, and abundant earthly life. The path to a heavenly Earth is what stirs within and what you act upon. Create love, act upon love, create compassion, act upon compassion, and together we will bring the cosmos one step closer to uniting in profound and infinite ways.

Enlightened Mavericks

People who have made the gifts of our Universal energy their study and their life's work, such as Edgar Cayce, Wendy Kennedy, John Edward, Sandy Anastasi, Kala Ambrose, stargazer Marguerite Manning, Lee Carroll, and Darryl Anka, have truly paved the way for others to continue the momentum for change. I know many of these mavericks personally and professionally and I am honoured to have been touched by their light and unique gifts of service. These teachers are authentic in every sense of the word and they have assisted in bringing Gaia into an awakened state.

Many of these mavericks have returned lifetime-after-lifetime to continue their soul's passion to assist the Divine in steering humanity to the light and the knowingness, within each of us, of the power we have to create brilliance.

If it had not been for these key people in my life who have encouraged me, and empowered me through their enlightened and authentic teachings and guidance, I would not be writing what I am today. The path they are on honours the highest aspect of the Divine and paves the way for those of us who desire guidance, to learn, but most of all to realize our innate link within one another in this profound earthly experience.

Their role in our increased understanding of the unseen world of energy is immeasurable. They have all had a profound effect on my life and I am indebted to their fearless commitment to inspire, empower, and educate humanity.

With each generation, I see more and more of these mavericks paving the way to free the light. Many star-seeds now are learning at a younger age what I only started to learn in my late thirties. We have the ability now, more than ever, to openly create portals through social media sites and other formal and informal groups to enable the greater expression of who we are.

Each person on this planet has the ability to create change for a better world and the best masters are the ones who encourage and empower the rest of us to rise up and become one of the teachers of tomorrow. With every thought and every heartbeat, change can occur and we can all co-creatively carve the path for others to set the stage for mass enlightenment.

Masters

It is within us all to walk the path that the Masters have walked, and in our own way. As we act within our pure love and authenticity, we allow our hearts to gift the world. This is the gift that all the Masters have given; the gift of their unconditional and unbridled love that is still written and mirrored to this very day. The gift of authenticity is truly that of freedom, and each Master served in an unwavering fashion because of their love for humanity. A true desire for humanity is to know freedom, to taste of pure Divine essence, and experience the link to Source that beats and pulses within us all. All of these teachings were based on the Masters' ability to walk with profound authenticity for who they declared and intended themselves to be.

We sometimes forget those who have walked and told their story in their own unique way. The many Masters who lost their lives to live in their truth is the underlying message that lingers within us all today. We, however, are awakening into the rebirth of our own master consciousness. To walk as the Masters walked and to do so with a profound alignment to Source, to Light, and to the Divine in which we were created. To be in oneness with all of Creation, all beings, all species, and all forms of life to bring us the freedom to walk a path that is as infinite and powerful as we are.

We all have the potential to carry ultimate benevolence for all life so that we can begin to walk the path of the Masters and understand the expansiveness for how Source perceives life. Source desires to know life from all aspects, all levels, all experiences, and that is all existence is anyway; experience. Our expanding and ascending consciousness is that of the path to Source, for the more we know life in all of its forms, the more we can begin our ascent ever closer to Source.

Empaths

There are pockets of empathic and intuitive beings, like myself, placed strategically all over the planet. As our playground expands with the potential from our combined desire to seek and know more, there are those quietly working in the front lines to balance and imbue wisdom, light, and love for all those who are attracted to it. As our collective grows in this planetary awakening, there will be greater potential for formal human guides to help newly awakened souls to being their alignment the expanding collective consciousness.

The energetically sensitive ones, among us, are tuning in and aligning with Gaia's vibrations and they are open to precognitive visions. They are experiencing the atunement and alignment of energy streams at global and collective levels. Some people even do this without knowing as evidenced by brilliant inventions or ideas that are inspired in dreams or out of the blue epiphanies. This is spiritual evidence that we are an aspect of a much grander orchestration and scheme. We are merely awakening to our power to create within it to direct the outcome with clarity, brilliance, and unlimited potential to a reality that is worthy of a 5th dimensional new Earth glow.

Self-Reflection

Desiring a life change is not enough; one must act and when we act upon our highest passion, we move towards our most authentic and Divine self. Ask yourself, in this calm and quiet moment, "How does living authentically look differently than how I am living now? How can I act on and incorporate one thing to align me closer to my higher truth, and ultimately better understand the spirit within? How can I act upon more intimate communications with those I encounter in my daily life, or honour myself in new ways, or honour others for their light? How can I act in accordance with the natural healing powers of Gaia, Source, to better align with my Divine path each day?"

It is by asking questions like these that can allow you to expand and extend who you are and what you are entangled with to contain a broader, Universal vibration. These practices and self-reflections can bring greater alignment to your Higher Self, your Divine plan and blueprint, and other higher dimensional beings that would love nothing more than to unify in Earth's growing acceptance of life forms outside its atmosphere.

These self-reflection questions will assist you in your ever-growing path to *know thyself.* Knowing who you are gives you greater clarity about the path you desire to align with. Your desire is the spark that lights the fire to create action, and action in perfect alignment with your authentic self, manifests miracles.

To desire a more fulfilling life is only one aspect of experiencing it and there are many things that require alignment before a dream can manifest. Action is required in all manifestation processes, and whether you desire a new car, a new home, a new career, or a new path with deeper meaning, it requires you to align with the vibration that matches that experience.

Change requires action and therefore, ascension is action towards your true natural self. Act in the direction of light and love of thy self and all will unfold with elegance and fluidity. The question is and has always been, "Is the desire potent enough for you to change what you are doing to experience something better?" What intent and vibration will you align to in order to take your life in the direction of your highest joy? Will you design your path and declare who you are to the Universe? What path will you carve for yourself and what destiny will you claim? What does your authenticity look like?

Intuition

Remember a time when you sensed something was about

to happen. Or when you had a sense about someone, or a place, or a decision you had made. Spirit, the innate steering mechanism that we all have encoded within, is our link to Source and the infinite, and we have been gifted with this tool to assist us in navigating a multi-dimensional reality. Perfect timing is the pace of spirit.

We will be given subtle whispers and tugs from spirit when it is time to walk the path of self-discovery. Events will unfold, keyed to the level of our readiness, and we will begin a series of events, circumstances, and occurrences that will allow us to act on our soul blueprints and life plans. The cues, clues, and subtle hints will become more profound and obvious until we take that step that heeds the call within. Our guides, our higher selves, the Universe, and all beings within Creation act in an elegant dance of quantum energy to deliver the magical events that can inspire us to remember who we are.

Acknowledge and embrace your power to intuitively navigate your way through this earthly experience. The more self-reflection and inner work you commit to, the easier navigating your way around subtle energies and preparing yourself for a 5th dimensional Earth will be. Like a spiral and the flower of life, you are forever unfolding, moving, expanding, and contracting with the natural ebb and flow of Creation. This is how our multi-dimensional innate aspect is intimately woven into our physical vessel and beyond into our auric and Merkabah aspects. We activate ever-heightened states of our infinitely expansive energetic body, or potential, to match that of our consciousness. We become more highly activated, thus allowing our senses to take on more information at a refined level.

All of this energetic interplay is unseen, but it can be felt. When you are inspired to go for a walk in a beautiful forest path, your cells, your innate aspect that resides within your cellular makeup, your creative senses, your physical vessel, your Akashic remembrances, all things that make up who you are, become activated in response to what Gaia is offering to you to tune into. If you walk with joy and intent to imbue yourself, engage yourself, entangle yourself within this experience, you will expand upon your Oneness with it. You will sense at the subtlest of levels that certain vibrations are not aligned with your newly heightened path, thus giving you the cue to move and shift.

Moving beyond the I AM aspect of understanding and living, and moving up into the I AM THAT I AM, presence. The All offers this to you in every breath you take. Our role is to tune in to it. In every way, this is how we rise up to meet those in already ascended status, and allow our highly activated wholeness to stretch beyond and merge with heightened potentials. This is how we prepare ourselves for higher resonated living.

We have all felt these inner warnings and sensations, and we can no longer deny the invisible intelligence that lies pulsing within us all. This is how energetic atonement and alignment will be a constant practice within your daily life and how we can alter and shift our path with each new thought. As the link within us strengthens, we then strengthen our connection within the Universe, our cosmic family, and All That Is.

Also, everything you experience is an offering from the Universe to know more deeply who you are, and all that you reside within, in a more expanded state. The Universe and the Divine are not superfluous. In each experience, there are lessons for us to expand. Every moment shows us at what level we resonate at and this experiential mirror is our most profound tool in assisting us to determine what frequency we are resonating at and if we desire to experience a new potential, we can then shift and alter from within to experience the effects of our new alignment.

We would not be given the ability to create or experience something if it were not possible to achieve it, so if you have a thought, inspiration, or creative musing, and you are excited to act upon it, then act. Trust your intuition.

The Higher Self

The Higher Self is the aspect of ourselves that decides with the Soul, on how, when, and why the choices and opportunities will occur for the physical aspect of who we are now. These are all predestined and designed by a myriad of beings. The Higher Self is intuitive, the medium, and the channel for it is the all-knowing aspect in the logistics of how to navigate through any reality we choose to experience. We are not cut off from Universal wisdom or any other intelligence of this higher aspect of who we are. In ascension and awakening, we can unveil more and more of the fluid path of communication to the Higher Self, for it is our greatest guide, and the higher aspect of us.

The link between the Soul and the Higher Self is one that is entangled in all lifetimes. This is why they are constantly feeding multi-dimensional energy to us to allow us the opportunities we need on our path. The Higher Self is the all-knowing driver, for it has the grander view of all the other lives, so it is the brilliant navigator in this energetic focus to direct us in all aspects of our lives. The Higher Self creates and assigns the appropriate beings, from a myriad of realms if need be, with the tasks and status updates of where you are at in our soul's blueprint, then the assignments are given for us to move forward on our paths.

Align your vibration to the experience you desire, live in the vibration of ecstasy, and tune into existence around you to sustain a continued process of realignment from what your reality mirrors to you. Trust that you have all you need to ride this wave and all will unfold as it was designed for you, by you.

Relax into the vibration of allowance, for there are many beings within a whisper ready to step up and assist all of us. Allow your physical self to sink into the knowingness of this elegant orchestration. The web of intertwined connections are enmeshed within the infinite and all that you need to experience will arrive exactly when you are ready for it. Our role is to align with ecstatic anticipation in unwavering trust that all of our inner light work and practice will allow the magical events to unfold in the highest and best form every time. Align, trust, practice, and allow.

Allowance is taking all of the above and imbuing it with love, for as you do this, you transform worry, doubt, fear, into profound self-love and expanded knowingness. Love is the highest vibration in our Universe and there is nothing it will not transform. You are an aspect of this Divinely perfect plan, so allow the state that you have set yourself and open to the gifts that will give you the confidence and illumination that your highest aspects knew would unfold for you.

The reason for our physical experience is to explore awakening in the most profound of ways and to consciously navigate our way to fulfil our soul's call; our blueprint in this unique life experience. We have all come here to experience the vibrational state of our true natural, Divine authentic self. It is in this natural state that we are able to express to Creation our won innate creativity. The soul level of our expression is the very centre of who we are and it is linked with Source — molecularly and energetically. This is why we are not just our physical structure; we are Divine essence and light.

Dreaming and Meditating

Dreams, meditations, and higher conscious states of being are all tools that enable us to explore the multi-dimensional aspects of who we are as well as other realms in order to better align with the frequency we desire. We can pull lessons, experiences, truths, and multi-dimensional wisdom from these experiences and then use them to further our energetic expansion and growth in this now experience.

Dreams are fluid and infinite, without borders or limitation. We can heighten these experiences by asking our team for clues to assist us, when we have a particular need, and have it delivered in our dreams or meditations. We will be awakened enough, during these times that we won't have to go into an altered state to receive wisdom from our guides. We can communicate with ease as we are already in a natural heightened state. We are given profound dreamtime and meditative experiences so that we can recall the relevant vibrations as we seek greater meaning and insight.

While in a dream or meditative state, energetic doorways open to us as we are in a heightened state of consciousness. And during such times, we are gifted with opportunities for expanded consideration that will bring us to a new level of understanding and resonance. In such heightened states as dreams or meditations, we fluidly release logic and doubt, and allow our teams to communicate with us in an unobstructed way. Our logical and analytical habits are placed in neutral and our spirit self is able to soar freely to work on our greater life path with the myriad of other beings that it takes to experience what we do.

As we unveil, understand, and integrate new information and frequencies, it is key to practice our newfound skills. Meditating is a quiet reflection time with your team, your multi-dimensional aspects, Gaia, nature, and so on.

Eventually, you will develop a skill to discern and interpret the symbols inherent in these experiences. It is important to journal these experiences in order to continue the flow of energy that is always moving through you and your reality. This process is key to continuing the energetic engagement and communication free flow in an expanded way.

The key attributes that will allow the constant flow of Universal energy to continue flowing to you in its diverse and magical ways are create, align, practice, trust, and allow. We all have the answers within us. So trust and allow what unfolds to deliver to you what needs to occur. Remember, spirit is benevolent and we are enmeshed within this grand orchestration of a beautiful Universal picture.

Merkabah

Merkabah is the name of our angelic essence — that is our energetic body, the vehicle through which we experience our expanded selves. It is a brilliant body of energy patterns, a reverberation of what you emit, what you design within your DNA and cellular makeup, and how it connects and relates to the Universe around and within you. It is an electromagnetic field of angelic consciousness through which we access our ability to activate all of these aspects of our higher selves so that we can vibrate in unison with all of Creation. The Merkabah is the Divine body through which we commune with the higher energetic realm and it expands as we expand.

The greater aspects of who we are may not be seen, but it is felt. When we experience inspiration, gut instincts, or life-altering sensations; this is the energetic communication between our energy and the higher energy of the Divine and it is sacred and loving guidance to help us navigate within this energetic existence.

All higher realm beings exist in the knowingness of energetic discernment and they communicate with us using tones, colours, light, telepathy, and pictographs. For humanity to ascend the lower vibrational realm, we must move beyond the limitation in our understanding about how to entangle and communicate as higher frequency beings and this requires learning to intuitively feel when we are 'going with the flow,' or have something to occur in 'perfect timing,' or with unexplainable *synchronicity* that is beyond any rational mindset. This higher vibrational communication through Merkabah allows us to move beyond the lower vibrational realm.

This is the ultimate lesson for humanity, to awaken to the

benevolence and communion between all lives within the Universe. May we all attain the awareness that living holistically and harmoniously is possible. This is a way for us to stay in balance; which is both our ultimate lesson and task.

These gifts and sensations that we experience through Merkabah, come from higher resonating beings and our awakening will ensure we are energetically ready and prepared for what is unfolding upon Gaia.

Lessons from Other Terrestrial Species

We have the opportunity to share our hearts and our love for Gaia with those non-humans with whom we share this planet, particularly those who are evidently conscious creatures, like the beautiful cetaceans in our oceans. Just as every human has a soul blueprint, so too do all the animal species upon our planet and like the multi-dimensional beings in lightships who offer stories that show they are entangled with humanity, so too does every species upon Gaia. Each animal that resides upon Earth has a lesson for us. These lessons bring us further insight about Creation.

Cetaceans, much like humans, have individual and

intelligent consciousness; furthermore, they are telepathic. They are engaged in a great work within our waters smoothing out and refining frequencies inundated our planet. Their purpose here is to communicate with the inter-dimensional consciousness about Gaia's resonance and to act as filters to transform incoming energy so it will benefit humanity. Smoothing out and refining negative and dark energy in a playful and healing way, their task is vital for our success.

All animals on this planet allow us to learn to love, honour, and get along with each other. All species within Creation have a unique story to tell and a unique vibration to offer. In these times of ascension, we have the opportunity to extend our awareness to include all species into an ideal in which we are all united on our shared planet as we usher in a truly golden era.

Chapter IX

Human Incarnation

The Physical Experience

Our most expanded, all knowing self, is our soul aspect, which resides within an even greater energetic aspect of the over-soul, and over-souls of over-souls and so on. In our pre-life planning experience, our spirit self, our spirit guides, and our planning teams, assisted in designing an agreements of themes and life experiences that will contribute to the overall evolution of our souls. Each life experience, indeed each life, has been maximized to allow for the greatest potential of growth and service.

And while our memories of this planning are veiled, we can ascertain the themes for this life by taking note of what situations and circumstances continue to surface in our lives that require us to stretch beyond our comfort zone, for these are usually clues to what we signed on for this time around.

Energetic and physical help always surrounds us, even if we

do not realize it. Information from Source and the angelic is sent through the soul self, based on what we are moving through and the overriding theme we are working on, and then fed to the Higher Self, spirit guides, and our celestial teams simultaneously. A grand energetic and multi-dimensional family all work together to offer, gift, and design this life experience for us to evolve in the highest manner possible.

When we first look at the bigger picture of expansion and ascension, we can begin to see the one act of uncovering more of who we were meant to be can ripple through to all of these other levels. And then it is obvious that the lessons we learn here are invaluable tools for many beings throughout Creation. We are physical examples of unique creative potential that can mirror back to all involved in our diverse and profound expression.

We have designed, at the highest levels, to cross-connect for the lessons required for either our growth and learning or the growth of those we come in contact with. All meetings, connections, and life-altering moments are perfectly timed by our soul and Higher Self, and like the process of ascension, there is nothing left out of this entanglement. We touch everything within Creation. This level and depth of understanding will become more and more prevalent as we move into greater exploration and communication with our celestial families. For every thought, emotion, and act, whether it be positive or negative in vibration, ripples through the cosmos and is felt throughout Creation.

Healing and Love

One of the steps in ascension is to bring to the surface all of our pains from every experience, in every lifetime, and in every dimension. We then have the opportunity to heal the grander aspect of our experience for greater good of the All. Healing may appear to occur within your life for you and those involved, but it spans to every dimensional plane that we are entangled within.

I remember coming to a moment of profound forgiveness when I witnessed the lives that I had lived in the time of Jesus, and the travesties and horrors that humanity experienced in the fear of what love could transform. I broke into tears and begged for healing from the highest light beings and God, for the death, injustice, and tremendous loss of life that we all experienced in those incredibly challenging times.

In times of great loss, whether you are on the other side of the planet, or the one being put to death, we all suffer, and the wounds of persecution and injustice resonate with us all in some way. Those of us who are extremely empathic and psychic carry the awareness in a more surreal way, thus the healing can be challenging and equally profound.

I know now through such experiences that grieving and releasing the energetic karmic imprints are incredibly healing and just as experientially real as if the experience happened last week. Energy is energy. We can transform and propel it, direct it, and build upon it, but it is always energy. Whether the trauma was an experience from a hundred lifetimes ago or on another realm, the healing must occur in some way. As you sense these emotions of time-lines you may not fully understand, or experiences you may not fully remember, they are all being brought to the surface for a reason, and quiet reflection time, meditation time, and a clear pathway to your spiritual team can assist you in releasing these multi-dimensional imprints.

There is healing in forgiveness and with forgiveness, there

is awakening into greater self-love. Like a natural energetic cycle within Creation, the more love we sense within ourselves, the more we want to experience. This is how expansion really occurs. Through the expansion of our awareness into greater vibrating beliefs and concepts, we unveil our natural Divine self, which is imbued with Source energy and unconditional love. This level of love transforms all within its path.

Our lives will slowly crave expanded ways to rediscover more of who we are so that we can in a sense fall back in love with who we truly are. Every being that resonates at the 5th dimensional level and above has a deep and intimate level of love for the self and the excitement to explore and expand upon the self also expands all within Creation. This is why self-love is so profoundly powerful and can heal any wound at any level.

The excitement to explore leads to the excitement of self-discovery, and greater self-discovery leads to greater and more expanded self-love, greater self-discovery, and greater self-love, thus perpetuating the whole Universal expansion cycle repeatedly to infinity and beyond. Love and light are expansive and it is also our natural state of being. When we commit to living in full authenticity, we tap into love's expansiveness to ever-greater depths. Love is the most powerful antidote for disharmony and unrest.

Self-Doubt

Negative inner thoughts and dialogues create beliefs that generates an energetic and physical imbalance that results in illness, disease, and can stagnate our soul growth. The frequency at which we set our inner dialogue can be the difference between living a fulfilling life or living an emotionally numb life. If we live in constant states of doubt and fear, we are keeping an entire realm of experience at arm's length. Fear and doubt breed disconnection.

Releasing self-doubt and moving into a frequency of pure excitement and intentional living requires us to not only create a deepened state of self-love and self-acceptance, but to let go of the beliefs we carried that held us back. Rarely is the pain and doubt that we feel, about others. Pain from within is a result of agreeing with negative and fearful beliefs and conditionings that make us feel unworthy. Regardless of what life experience you have chosen, or what you feel others have done to you, we can honour the power that resides within all of our cells and break free to create a path resonant with our most adventurous of dreams. We create and co-create every experience in our lives, and we are not victims of circumstance.

As we take an honest assessment of every challenging and dark experience in our lives, we will see that the frequency we had set is what allowed us to manifest a particular situation into existence. Letting go of doubt and self-depreciating behaviours involves altering the beliefs we have that created these experiences in the first place. Greater awareness and forgiveness allows us to open our heart centre and create a pathway to climb out of the numb and darkened pit in which many of us have lived within for far too long.

Self-reflection and meditation is an excellent tool to unveil the beliefs that led to the feelings of diminished self-worth and the resulting pain. Remember too, some of the wounds we carry today can also be the karmic scars from other lifetimes. Energy can be carried in this way, and as all is happening simultaneously, the psychically sensitive people sometimes toggle the pains from other lifetimes as current triggers pull in the energetic memories. This is the reason we sometimes experience feelings of despair and anger even though there is no apparent reason to feel this in our current reality. The wounds are bleeding through from another frequency for us to heal in this now moment. Some of these scars and wounds still resonate and will do so until we heal them with love and forgiveness within this now.

Releasing self-doubt and any other negative and painful beliefs, requires that you first acknowledge it, embrace what you unveil, then allow it the honour of bringing you to a place of heightened knowingness and clarity. In this process alone, you release it to the cosmos to be transformed into love. We then have the potential to redefine ourselves with beliefs and definitions that are more powerful and beauty so we can walk forth in surety, clarity, and self-honour for our ability to create, realign, and rise up.

Courage

Our innate encoding to walk any path in the desire to satisfy our insatiable curiosity is why many of choose to take on roles that seem at the time to be eccentric or unorthodox. We have experienced every tragedy, every elation, every challenge, and every life turmoil. Despite this, we manage to find the courage to walk a path that few will desire to take. We access incarnations that appear to be steeped in limitation and fear, perhaps for the thrill of the ride when our souls ricochet with the power of releasing the final remnants of self-doubt and lack as we transcend into a new illuminated state. We are taking the chance that we will emerge and blossom as we are inspired with the elixir of Source surging through our veins, and the love that permeates every ounce of our being-ness. We must have courage to see past the illusion and take it on for the benefit and desire of Creation to expand from Universe to Universe and planet to planet as we take on life roles to help in whatever way we can — and so the light will prevail.

Our efforts to sync within our own Divine plan; we will catalyse our planet and ultimately bring our collective vibration up to create a light quotient that will be seen and felt as it ripples throughout Creation. Our soul plans will require that we let go of the standard and garner the courage necessary to carve a bold path toward the ultimate truth.

Self-Empowerment

This amazing energetic shift that's being amped up with every seasonal and cosmic alignment continues to serve us in many ways. It allows us the opportunity to further explore the genetic encoding that can be activated in these increased amplifications. If we allow the triggers to release learning opportunities, we can see the lesson within each experience and transcend it. We have the creative ability to see the power within each lifetime and to transform our limitations and pains by creating an expanded way to alter the frequency that we generated when the experience first occurred.

As we move along our path of ascension, we can see how our vibrations mirror our experiences and we will be amazed when we look back at particularly challenging or even profound moments and see the links that tied our state of being to these experiences.

Something similar is happening to our collective energetic state. As opposing energies jockey for position, there will be a shaking out of anything that does not align with the collective's desires. And as there is a movement toward freedom and ascension, those energies will prevail. Our collective is examining eons of persecution, confinement, death, and injustice. There is a lot of suppressed energy locked in the vibration of victimization.

It is Universal law — what we emit, we attract. To release the power of victimization, we must create reflective time to allow the depths of these scars, pains, and traumas to surface and ultimately be transformed into self-empowerment.

We are only responsible for our paths and regardless of how the pain originated, we can create profound knowingness and escape that pain, even pain that was inflicted upon us by others. Awareness is the key to enlightenment, self-love, self-honour, and ascension and awareness will also allow us the compassion for those who walk a different path.

The frequency emanated from those dwelling in a state of victimization is linked to the sense that the victim has no choice. However, once we acknowledge and embrace all aspects of who are, even our darkest aspects, we can heal. Negative frequencies are generated from those parts of us that we have not yet acknowledged and loved. Fear is the absence of love, so offering love to the darkness and fear will enable us to love ourselves into wellness, beauty, and infinite creative light.

As we move through these healing tasks, we refine and re-tune our frequency, and we literally lighten up and speed up. Our cellular processes shift with our newfound knowingness and we become lighter, freer, and more exuberant. In honour of our multi-dimensionality, we join the benevolent resonance of our celestial family.

The Law of Attraction

Everything within Creation carries a vibration. For everything is energy, and energy is everything. Just as there is personal ascension and expansion, so too does this relate to collective, planetary, galactic, and Universal evolution. Within every level of Creation, there are frequencies that resonate in accordance with its environment.

If we know what it is we desire to manifest, then it is a matter of 'being' the vibration of that experience to see it unfold before us. There is always a much grander playing field for everything we know to be true, and we are entangled within it all. All is valid in our search for higher meaning and expanded living.

We have the potential here to create something from nothing and sense our true profundity as Divine creators. The Law of Attraction is simply the Universal law in which we attract to us the direct vibration of what we emit. Everything within Creation has a vibrational signature and to manifest anything, we need to align ourselves to the frequency. The Law of Attraction is one of the key attributes of this earthly incarnation and to fully understand our greater picture, as humanity evolving, and within an ascending planet, we need to look at our current vibrational state.

To manifest an earthly experience in which our world encapsulates harmony and health at all levels is the role we aspire to as newly illuminated galactic humans. We must first create the awareness that this is possible, and then, we encapsulate every opportunity that feeds this manifestation.

Everything is energy and our world is a direct reflection of what we, the collective are resonating. If we desire a healthy, strong, and balanced planet, with the offering of healthy water, soil, and air, then we must manifest this vibration from within first. We are raising our frequency so that we can match that of other ascending planets and learn our way into creating a new Earth that can sustain life for an infinite period for her life blueprint.

You can be tuned into a channel that's negative and untrusting, or you can emit profundity in all you think, say, and do. Whatever belief drives you in life will be the mirror of what you experience in your reality. This is a Universal Law.

What you put out will be exactly what you experience.

This is not a lofty idea nor is it guesswork. It is the Universal Law that has long been taught in the Mystery Schools, temples, and by shamanic leaders in countless ancient tribes. These teachings were brought to those in vibration to understand, revere, and propel these Universal gifts that were brought from the star systems of the Pleiades, Sirius, and even Arcturus and seeded within the hearts and minds of those devout to Universal entanglement.

Living Authentically

Authenticity is the core essence of who we are in the eyes of Source. Underneath the myriad layers of conditions, beliefs, and assumptions about who we are within the illusory reality we live within, this is our true authentic self. Each authentic self is unique, like an energetic fingerprint, or stamp, and is unique to each person. Authenticity is crucial as an energetic vibration as it can allow us to be steered in the right direction as we move through our awakening, and in many ways, it allows us to solidify who we are to the Universe and within the energetic stream of Gaia.

Authenticity allows us to not only rediscover who we are as spirit essence, but it allows us a richer taste for the life we designed to create. Authenticity is the pathway to the heart and provides an open door for others to experience us at a more intimate level. Authenticity opens the portal to the Divine and just as being ecstatic, or being in love can breathe new light within our lives, so too does being our most authentic self. As we emit authenticity from our heart, the electromagnetic pulses are sent out to Creation and then are brought back to us in the same vibrational match to mirror to us what we are capable of. This means that we attract those that are in a perfect match with our authentic vibration, and we can know that as we become more and more authentic, we resonate with those who are also acting within their true authenticity. This is the perfect design in which the Universe works, energetically allowing all within Creation to find its true perfect match for that energetic experience.

Not only do we attract others that also act within their authenticity, but also we attract situations and potentials of our infinite creative brilliance. This level of allowance and energetic alignment gives us a free pass to tap into creative talents from any realm that may enhance our current expression and experience. You can see this example of talent being transferred or triggered with some of the child prodigies born over the past twenty years. Some have referred to these children as *star-seeds* or *indigo* children and have innate creative abilities that would seem to be unusual for children their age.

We have all had experiences when we feel out of alignment to our authentic frequency. We have all met people at a party, celebration or work gathering, and the situation feels fake or contrived. We may have even felt as if we were the ones acting fake or out of alignment with our true authentic selves, and the moment we alter who we are to meet the demands of others or to mesh with or fit in with those you simply do not vibrate in resonance with, it feels contrived and inauthentic.

Pay attention to these feelings, as you will always be guided to alter your behaviour so that you can realign with what feels authentic. We have all experienced moments where we alter who we are to act more in alignment with others, and it never has lasting appeal. You are perfect, you are required, and as you offer exactly who you are to the Universe, you allow the Universe a clear path to find for you all the experiences you truly desire to attract.

However challenging it may be to be authentic, it will in the result in more favourable outcomes because you will attract and align yourself with those who are a true match to your frequency. If we play the role of other's vibration, or align with other's behaviour then we are only attracting a small portion of our true potential. It is not authentic if you are following someone else's path. Authenticity means that you honour, embrace, own, and allow, the unique sheen that you have to offer to flow forth and stand firm in your own design. What a beautiful story this authentic self can paint for the Universe and it is your story to tell! Authenticity opens the door to greater ecstasy and joy as it is directly aligned with your Higher Self, your heart's desire, and your celestial team to which you are preparing to meet.

Living Ecstatically

The power of positivity and the alignment with the energy of happiness allows us to manifest many things. The path of ascension is about this alignment as it unveils our true higher and natural Self. All of the concepts that are revealed on the path of awakening allow us to draw on and reflect upon what 'feels' right in the here and now. The ability to connect all that has been learned, unveiled, and uncovered enhances our deeper connection with what we will know to be possible. The Divine self, the Higher Self, and all other multi-dimensional aspects that concurrently co-exist on other levels of vibrational platforms, can all co-mingle and enhance each another. In this enhancement, we allow our multi-dimensional brilliance to shine as we celebrate in the unity that we have created.

As we go about our daily life, it is important to be aware of our state of mind as this is what is projected out to Creation. This doesn't mean that we have to over manage or even micro-manage our emotions, but it does mean that we need to create powerful reflection time that and we need to check-in occasionally to check and alter our frequency settings, as needed. As we touch base with our inner aspects, we build a path to our Divine and Higher Self and open the portals to higher frequency vibrations and their associated opportunities, synchronicities, and other magical potential. With each new level of integration of our ascension learning, we expand to a higher realm of experience and lessons.

With every breath, we are accepting and altering our own life force. If we have refined our beliefs and walk with boldness in who we are, then living ecstatically and with Divine purpose will flow naturally. Breathe in the essence of your boldest and profound self.

Living ecstatically and with excitement and joy, allows us to further amp-up our frequency in unlimited ways. We have infinitely innate powers within that have been unavailable to us merely because we have not been in the vibration to see it or experience its profundity. The process of awakening is the process of expanding our thinking beyond what has been to what can be. The commitment and love that we imbue for our self, will help us explore and experience all that we are capable of creating and instructing within our life in the grandest of ways. Self-love and self-honour brings us in alignment with the vibration of a new level of experience called *ecstasy*, the frequency that allows a 5th dimensional consciousness and all that can unfold within this vibration in alignment to us.

Ecstasy is the energetic channel or station that allows the portals of infinite possibility to be opened to us. As we co-create our earthly experience as a collective, we each create our own specific reality. The ability to align ourselves with whatever vibration we desire is the primary tenet that gives us permission to know what is possible. Any vibration we desire is available to us and if we align to these vibrations with our thoughts, beliefs, definitions, and emotional purity then all things are possible.

Ecstasy is a profound vibration and is directly linked with unconditional love. For the ability to tap into the vibrational channel of ecstasy, we must love ourselves enough to allow us to feel and experience it. Ecstasy aligns us with our highest and best selves. It is the path of the Divine and all higher realm vibrations. Ecstasy brings us into the portal of possibility that connects into the vibration of our Higher

Selves, which in turn aligns us with opportunity and events to further our progress down the path. The love that our higher self, our spirit guides, and our celestial team have for us is the vibration of ecstasy and opportunities will come our way as we increasingly resonate in these vibrations.

Ecstasy is the link to everything within our cosmos and Universe. There is no concept of separation within ecstasy. If we intend to fill every aspect of ourselves with the vibration of ecstasy, then we are in alignment with the energetic stream of Gaia and everything within Creation. We are preparing ourselves to let go of all that is old and limiting and then allowing ourselves to slip into the profound potential of who we were created to be.

This ecstatic alignment sets us up on a path that supports heightened manifestations. The vibration of the ecstasy channel offers an infinite array of experiential options. It is in this vibration that we can attract anything within the infinite. When this happens, excitement will unfold in all that we do and in seamlessly perfect in timing. Our multi-dimensional existence allows us to sense, experience, and feel a multitude of dimensional frequencies. We can commune and enmesh with our divine and authentic self, as we ascend into higher vibrational living.

This is not something we need to work for to obtain; it is our natural essence. We are all spirit essence, and we have the potential to slip into remembrance as we live within the vibration of ecstasy. As we unveil the layers of conditionings and beliefs that have lock us in the old energy frequencies, we uncover our true authentic and ecstatic selves. There is no reason to worry, doubt, fear, or micro-manage our lives and struggle for survival as we have for much too long, for what aligns us with all that we desire is and always has been within. The path ahead, dear lighted ones, is one that is set in the moment of now and to the highest frequency we can muster until each and every day is naturally flowing in ecstasy. This is the vibration to set our 5th dimensional channel to as it is imbued with the knowingness that we are worthy of the self-love it mirrors back. The brilliance of ecstasy is within us right here and right now.

A Natural State

Flowing with universal energy is what we were created to do naturally. We have been separated from our energetic senses for so long that we now have to relearn how to tune in and align. Your true natural self is the one you designed to explore when you entered this earthly incarnation. The more fluidly we flow with the natural essence of the Universe, as we tune in to what we experience, the more we allow ourselves to unfold, unfurl, and slip into our natural higher aspects. This alignment opens the door to higher aligned synchronicities, and eventually, multi-dimensional communications and visitations. When we flow with who we are naturally and authentically, we allow our senses to see what has always been in front of us.

Remembering your true natural state will occur as you continue along your path with excitement and passion. You have encoded within you, based on what you designed within your life blueprint, the triggers that will initiate excitement, joy, love, passion, and other higher vibrational feelings when you tap into your gifts. These are your cues to align with your highest and best path and will always guide you if you are tuned in to what you feel and what beliefs you hold. This is why it is key to create reflective time each day in order to refine your beliefs and definitions to change and shift as you do. You designed such triggers to wake you up in the appropriate moment. It is important to follow the physical and emotional signs that arise. The more we connect with these ancient inner workings of our Universe, the more we can create clarity in defining and designing our powerful path.

As we align, tune in, and reconnect with our natural state, we can experience the pure elegance of the Universe. All That Is gifts everyone in incredible ways and when we are aligned enough to connect with it, we expand farther and higher. This alignment starts with being exactly who we signed on to be, regardless of the challenges that appear to hold us back. When our alignment and remembrance unfolds, we create profound excitement and joy as we feel like we finally fit.

In full recognition of our infinite potential as spiritual beings, we seek heightened experiences, further entanglement, and a grander look at all things and it can only be achieved if we unfold and honour our divinely authentic natural self. Judgements, conditions, and separation, and any other limiting aspects will fall away because we have tasted the joy of freedom in who we truly are. How powerful is this?

We can create all of these experiences by shifting and

aligning to who we were meant to be and more importantly, who we designed ourselves to be. It is the contract with ourselves that we are manifesting and fulfilling. Synchronicity always allows us the opportunity to alter and shift our perceptions, our definitions, and our beliefs to experience our highest and best at all times. It is up to us to tune in and rise up.

Physical or Spirit Essence

We are not physical beings having dreams; we are spirit essence experiencing a dream of being physical. The illusions that we create in every aspect of our physical lives are evidence enough that we really do have the power to create anything. The moment you awaken to an expanded view of your reality, you will shift the potential from merely existing within structured confines with rules, and open the doors of the infinite that delivers miracles of potential.

Dreaming our reality and awakening in the dream of a 5th dimensional new Earth is expanding to the point where both realities merge and where the multi-dimensional experiences no longer have to be presented in these heightened states, for we have become the heightened state of consciousness. If we are powerful enough to dream this physical existence, or create it, then what expansive things are we able to tap into?

We are all energetic consciousness at various levels, resonances, and states of being, and we have created all these aspects of physicality to serve in our process to awaken, expand, and grow. In a co-creative collective agreement, we exist with others who are also dreaming this experience and all agreements are entangled within one another. We are being gifted with energetic alignments and triggers that assist us as we emerge from this dormant sleep allowing us a glimpse that our reality is not what we thought.

All realities exist at various levels of consciousness as web-like and layered energetic patterns that is just a hologram within a hologram, within the infinite, all co-existing within this same, now moment. It is our consciousness that creates the experience that becomes a reality. It can be conceivable, then, that we are creating this reality in the same manner as we create the dreams that dazzle us at night, and it is the level of awareness and the intent to which we create within this awareness that creates our experiences. We don't have to be in a waking state of disconnection to everything in our reality, but shift our perspective to being the creator of this version of a dream. We are literally waking up within the dream that is this reality.

Try to grasp the concept at the spirit level and then honour the true power and incredible focus that we already own as we have created the illusions that we exist within. However, the key to remember is that we have this power and we must allow ourselves to wake up to it and start living and reengaging with life again. We can remember all potentials and like a pulsar that beams to infinity and beyond, we are immediately shifted to the reality where miracles occur because we have shifted our knowingness to match this potential.

Chapter X

5th Dimensional Consciousness

Alignment

As we move into ascension, and into higher states of awareness, we act more clearly on what we feel, as opposed to what we think. We understand that the communion between the Higher Self, the spirit self, the soul self, and our physical body self, is remembering how to interact and co-mingle once again, as awakened spirit beings. Energetic alignment is the tuning in process to what we feel as we hone our senses to such a degree that we instinctively *know* what feels like when we are in spiritual alignment to a desired state of being.

Alignment will become second nature as we continue to tune in to every moment. It is possible to consciously create how we desire to feel. We have ultimate power to set the frequency on every word and circumstance that we experience. Alignment is the process of achieving oneness within the moment. Misalignment can be determined in moments of reflection and meditation and once the seeker releases the belief that is causing the blockage, we will actually feel the shift as we move into alignment with Source.

We can sense the energy of others, the energy of Gaia, Source energy that resides within as we centre and align with unconditional love, and our cells, our body, reacts to it all. We are like physical antennae and have the potential to link in with everything. We steer our vessels toward the frequency that inspires and delights us. Our physical body will always show us when to move closer, or move away. Excitement and joy allows us to steer in the right direction and to further practice and hone our innate communication and intuitive skills, as well as our ability to merge with the environment. Our bodies are alive with cellular knowingness and a state of conscious design that desires to be in tune with the rest of its entangled systems.

Alignment is about feeling our way into ascension by always pointing and guiding our hearts to sense pleasure, love, and light, and then allowing all to unfold in perfect timing and delight. Align with confidence, align with compassion, align with tolerance, align with health, align with abundance, align with wisdom, align with Universal oneness, and so on. All paths to profound unveiling begin with who we design and define ourselves to be in every moment. There is no need to plan outline our goals in this. All that is necessary is to allow ourselves the maximum potential of this now moment by being clear about who we are and what we desire to experience. Align with this frequency and we will see our realities shift.

If a situation calls for tact, compassion, and inner reflection, then define yourself as loving, compassionate, tolerant, and forgiving. Each moment, each thought, each situation is an opportunity to align with our highest and best selves. It may feel at first to take a lot of effort, but we will find that if we commit to this process for even one day, a practiced consciousness will form for us. We are the masters of our vessels and potential.

As our planetary environment shifts with new and refined streams of atmospheric light, our whole aspect will naturally slip into the flow of the offering, like a beautiful elixir of Source essence, coalescing and cohesive as if it were one and always meant to be there. We do not need to struggle in our lives, we merely need to get clear about who we are, let go of who we are not, and align with an amped-up frequency because of our intentional process to define clearly, who we are within this elegant Universal system.

In our natural state, we are energetic beings and all energy must flow. It must be fluid and free. Energy must be in alignment to the desired state in order to produce what we desire to experience. If our beliefs and definitions are weak or negative, then not only will what we attract be a vibrational match in this way, but the whole aspect of who we are will only attain what we direct or program it to. Program your whole being to a profound state of being and you will start to vibrate at this rate and as the Earth changes, there will be greater cohesion and clarity for what you are truly capable.

Alignment is constant and continual, and like adjusting the radio to a new hit station that plays only the top hits, so too can we program our lives and bodies. Why experience negativity, or doubt, or fear, or struggle, or strife, of lack of self-worth, if we do not have to? We can intermingle with the intelligence of spirit if we align to its frequency and bring a greater awareness to all aspects of who we are as we expand in new directions and heightened states. The purity of intent and passion about who we are will be the fuel that propels the Universe to provide us with the gifts that respond to the frequency you emit. The illuminated galactic human that will one day have the capability, skill, and provision to exist within these heightened arenas of advancing worlds and this is what our bodies are preparing for now.

Surrender

Knowing you are so profoundly loved, truly appreciated, and valued that you receive gifts of synchronicity delivered each and every time, will help you to flow with the vibration of the Divine. We desire this intimate link with one another, the brilliant dance of synchronicity that only energetically directs itself based on what we align ourselves to. It is a Divine, energetic dance and we are the lead dancer. The more open, aware, and acknowledging of all aspects of this magical Universe that we are all swimming within, the more we will begin to taste this web of golden layers of Source essence, intelligence, and love.

Surrender to your brilliance as a profound creator within

the Divine environment of potential. Surrender to the potential that you are able to create anything you desire with your growing awareness. As your consciousness expands, you rise up in vibrational settings and align with synchronicity that will bring you to a state of astonishment every time. Surrender is your gift to the Divine in which you offer your trust, your gratitude, and your appreciation for the life you have been given.

Remembrance

Planetary ascension, with the unconditional assistance of our multi-dimensional friends and family, is a journey into remembrance in which we will experience a reality that flows with the ease and our ability to connect with the expansiveness of who we are as infinite energetic beings will be our reality. Remembrance is the ultimate reward. We will re-learn how to travel inter-dimensionally, to spontaneously heal, and extend our lifespans, and manifest anything we desire with just a thought.

Our celestial family awaits to extend these teachings to us and remind us of the power we hold within. As we become reunited with our immense consciousness and energetic intelligence, we open ourselves up to the inter-stellar wisdom that many ascended planets already live by. The Universe will be open to our exploration and discovery and we will remember our engagement with Gaia so that harmony, balance, and a healthy eco-system can be sustained. How utterly grand is this experience? Purely magnificent!

Ascension is our return to our more whole selves in the highest and most loving aspect. This is the path to remembrance so we can fulfil our soul's purpose and our passion for growth and new experiences. The more we expand in our mindset and thoughts, the more our infinite potential becomes our new reality. We will remember our true essence as aspects of the creator, as pure, uninhibited, unlimited, and with infinite energetic potential

In these magnificent times, in each moment, we can release our obsession with time and any other physical restrictions and limitations; we allow the freedom of infinite potential to entangle with our core vibration to become active co-creators. From the earliest of humanity's experience, we have learned how destructive of greed and misused power over others can be and we are now ready to liberate ourselves from these evils.

By engaging in inner seeking, we can finally expand into a sense of true freedom and enlightenment for the first time. We can know our most expansive aspects and engage once again with our family among the stars from which we came. We are profound magnetic energetic beings and what we attract and manifest will be the frequency that we emit. We are more than this physical body and physical brain. We are energetic, infinite, and immense. As we ascend, we'll begin to see and experience this fact.

When we allow ourselves to ask, to seek, to listen, and to act on the path of light, inquiry, and expansion, we can then begin to understand the deepest sense of who we are. In this profound remembrance, this process of ascension, we can breathe life back into our beloved Gaia for Her very life depends upon it.

We have always been sent unconditional love, guidance, and assistance from a myriad of beings from all corners of the Universe. They continuously guide and assist us from the directives and excitement as outlined in their own soul blueprints and from the auspices of Source. There are a diverse and infinite number of beings involved with the Divine plan for Gaia's ascension and they serve in benevolence and joy.

In knowing how infinite and powerful we are and how ultimately profound our expansiveness is, how can we merely sit back and do nothing? We are finally taking our places upon this grand stage for the first act in this magnificent play within the Universal story of ascension. Our task is to expand our thoughts, our beliefs, and our innate sense of being to open up to the forthcoming energy. It is within us to ask, to seek, and to listen for our spirit is always calling and our soul is always designing new opportunities for us to act upon.

Know with conviction that you are far greater than you may imagine right now. Even if you cannot see it or feel it at this time, trust and allow your sensate ability to guide you to the next step in awakening. For if you ask, it will be given — always. If you seek, you will find, and if you trust, you will flow. Surrender into the knowingness of who you were meant to be and explore the inner whispers that your spirit softly sends. As we expand into new heights of personal awareness and Universal understanding, we empower one another to awaken into remembrance of our innate infinite potential, returning to our profoundness. These stirrings will allow us to step up into our illuminated galactic human resonance and role within our greater cosmic family.

Higher Vibrational Living

This accelerated time of awakening is due to all the energy workers who have come to us from all over the galaxy to increase the power of the positive energy vibrations. Their unconditional love and energy patterning is a sacred gift to us and is evident, not only in the sensations we feel from the energy fields, but in the synchronicities that reveal the connections between each of us and with Source, Gaia, and Creation.

Our soul's story is like a puzzle that falls together miraculously. And even before we consciously begin to align, we will be able to feel deep within ourselves just how profound our potential for growth is. And once we are awakened, we can use our expanding awareness to sense our way through the subtle changes in our lives as we shift and raise our vibration to higher core states of beliefs and thoughts.

Higher vibrational living means we can create and manifest far more instantly than ever before and our senses may open enough for some to become channellers and scribes to assist in the dispensation of higher realm beings, information, and wisdom. We all have the ability to tap into the abilities we carry in other parallel realities to offer in this reality. Even more, we can promote the ascension of Gaia and our fellow humans by altering the awareness of the collective, for we are all linked, connected, and feeding off of the energy we all emit. Like a cosmic electric ball of light, what we emit, is released and touches all that you are entangled with.

A multi-dimensional being is one that has access to an infinite storage house of information, in a multitude of dimensional frequencies that can serve us at any time we choose. We are not only a physical body. We have greater aspects of ourselves that sense, inspire, guide, and direct our life's purpose. Our over-soul is the greater aspect from which it is the holder of a myriad of souls within the soul collective and within which our individual souls reside. It is derived from the over-soul of over-souls all the way to the All That Is.

Living as a multi-dimensional being means that there is an understanding of who and what we are expanding within, and how energetically entangled we are with all that exists. To create a myriad of experiences that allows us to tap into any dimensional realm, or potential, is about being the master of our energetic frequency.

5th Dimensional Energetic Expression

I now understand that ascension must be experienced as a progressive template. The dispersing experience was given to prepare me for the work that I will be putting forth here, but also the aspects of the myriad of other realms that I am a part of. We are all energetic patterns and only our experience of this form is real. Our creator skills manifest a focus of spirit energy that is so profound it literally creates the illusion of all that we experience. We have all agreed to adhere to specific rules, laws, and limitations that govern this level of vibrational living. As we ascend, however, the rules and laws that govern our ability to space travel, experience multi-dimensional realms and beings, will become more flexible and malleable. We will be able to create with greater flow and even have the ability to experience other energetic realms with our expanding consciousness, returning to a physical form experience at will. Higher realm beings do not require physical crafts to visit us. They have the potential and ability to dematerialize or bi-locate instantly by their intent. We are shown lightships because it serves as a reminder to us that we are not alone and we never have been.

We will be able to experience a more diverse and multi-dimensional reality as we gain greater capacity to integrate each step that we move into. This progressive application of energetic self-discovery and integration is a natural unfurling of our illumination into an expanded version of the human species. These aspects are all required to explore, expand upon, and imbue as we prepare and align with the experiences that will allow us to finally reunite with our historical truths, our unlimited potential, and our celestial family in all of their glorious forms and states. A 5th dimensional new Earth will open and delight in open contact, and encourage the comings and goings of our greater celestial family, for there will be no limits, boundaries, or governments to hide behind or be deceived by.

We are finally remembering our ability to reconnect at the energetic level and create our realities. As we expand our infinite potential in awareness, understanding, and ability, we discover how our consciousness is the ultimate tool for creating possibilities. Our consciousness is a tool like no other within Creation. As we allow ourselves to expand our thoughts, our desires and our imagination. We set the stage for our consciousness to tap into cosmic knowledge and wisdom. Our teams then align and encourage, support, and prepare the playing field in which we design and create. Our consciousness is infinite and it is divinely encoded with greatness. The question is, will we steer our awareness with excitement and exploration, or will we hide behind a veil of limitation? We have freewill to do whatever it is that stirs us from within and knowing how truly unlimited we are can set the stage for profundity to unfold. Energy has no boundaries, and when we ignite our intent, our emotional readiness, and the love and purity of the heart, there is no distance over which our light will not emit.

Our consciousness is the vehicle in which all possibility can unfold. As each person awakens, the collective consciousness is also offered potentials from the Universe and the cycle of energy continues and remains in a more balanced state. As Gaia ascends, we will be offered these possibilities as well, but we do have to act. Allowing for open dialogue, open learning, and expanding into new areas of thought, potential, and discovery are all key attributes of expanding our level of consciousness and readying ourselves for ascension and contact. Every human at some point will desire to expand and evolve, for it is encoded within the very cells that make up who we are.

Those who are ready will find themselves reading books like this one, or taking a class, or starting meditation, and so on. It is an energetic dance, transference, an elegant intermingling within this web-like and infinite structure of benevolent systems within Creation. As we open our unique potential to its vast array of landscapes, we will be shown what will appeal to our unique soul's blueprint. It is our path, the lifeline that we are inherently moving on, that brings us in greater vibrational alignment to Source, of which we are all a part.

Experiencing the Multi-verse

The Universe is the All, and the All is the Universe. As we expand in our process of ascension, we expand our mindset to the greater, grander, aspect of creation. We can sense the connection with the 'All That Is,' and our role within it. Within expanded understanding, we can then see that there may not be only one singular Universe, but an infinite number of Universes. All Universes could possibly co-exist in this layering fashion. One Universe layered upon one another, enmeshed and interwoven. Each Universe has its own Divine plan that unfolds, and its own themes to play out.

Just as there are a variety of planets within our galaxy, so too are there vibrational rules that each planet within the galaxy has chosen to play within. Just as every human being has its soul plan, so too do each planet and galaxy within the Universe. Everything within our Universe has meaning and purpose, and even if we do not recognize the elegance within these profound multi-dimensional meanings, it still exists and offers a story to all other beings about its unique expression and role within the greater whole. Whatever you can imagine is somehow real in some aspect of your being. Every planet has the potential to sustain life often in frequencies that we are simply unable to detect.

To gain access and ability to expand into other realities at will, it is key that we live fully in this moment of now. All potentials, all opportunities are always offered now, and as we imbue all of the now with whom we are authentically, the ability to manoeuvre where ever we desire can be given its freedom to unfold. This is how mastery unfolds, and it is always an elegant dance of potential and knowingness of what already exists as we rise up in frequency to experience it. There is great richness within each and every experience.

Practicing to resonate in this now moment is a very powerful shift in the perception of what's possible and how this one shift in your beliefs about time and space can take you to new levels of experience.

To experience this multi-verse and the infinite aspects of our multi-dimensional self, we need to shed the beliefs and definitions we have about time, space, and the extensive limitations we have about who we believe ourselves to be and what we exist within. Our reality is much more flexible than we have ever been taught, and as we expand, we will experience time anomalies. As we physically speed up, the acceleration within our cells will create a sense of timing that coincides with the directives in our soul blueprint, and the blueprint for Gaia and Creation.

To do this, it is essential to take time for quiet, solitary, meditative reflection every day. Meditation allows a power of stability to enable us to feel centred as we ride the tides of chaos in these drastically changing times. As we move into more of our energetic selves, we become aware of the greater aspects of who we are, and what those other aspects require from us to remain in a state of homeostasis.

Our Higher Self, our soul, our spirit self requires that alignment so that all states and aspects have their full ability and potential to shine. Like the rays of light piercing through a prism, or the spectrum of a rainbow, or a beautiful kaleidoscope, all contain their own specific design and colourful attributes to their overall richness of the whole. We are tapping into the many beautiful hues that humanity really is and it starts with embracing our true authentic self.

If we create time each day to listen, and actively align to our higher consciousness states, we not only remember our uniqueness, but we remember how to reengage and reconnect with our spirit essence and Oneness with Source. As we hone our innate energetic abilities and senses, we will prime our soul for optimal resonance and service.

If we do not allow our authentic self, our spirit essence to shine, we will begin to feel unbalanced, stifled, uncertain, and compressed with energy because we are blocking the energy from flowing in a natural and Divine way. We may even feel carried away with the chaos (rather than surfing the waves of that chaos), because we lack the grounding and centeredness of who we truly are within the whole. Spiritual practice brings greater self-clarity and allows us to let go of all doubt and fear, which in turn unfolds a greater view on what truly is.

The more practice one takes in honing these innate abilities, the greater level of trust is gained and the greater potential is realized. We have such potential to traverse the portal into what we desire to experience and as we expand, we will be afforded this exciting opportunity. Remember, the level of expansion that we allow our consciousness and awareness to unfold is directly related to what opportunities we are able to manifest for ourselves.

We can experience energetic shifts of awareness that will come in the form of impressions, dreams, or even waking conscious thoughts, feelings, or sensing about what we experience on other planets and in other realms. The more we create quiet reflection and meditation time in our everyday life, the more we will start to experience multi-dimensional gifts that will ground and expand upon our here and now experiences. If we are not using each of these profound experiences to expand all that we are in the now of this reality, then we are not benefiting from the entire purpose of the event. Remember, there are no accidents so if you are experiencing something; there is a lesson, a reason, or a higher purpose to why it is unfolding. There is always a lesson within the challenges and darker experiences as well, in that they can bring about healing and expansion to serve in the now and they can bring about celebration, honesty, self-love, self-expression, and improvements to our higher authenticity.

The Star Council

The Star Council is a mediation, ambassadorial council of a collective of twelve planets within our local Universe. They offer their services, guidance, and historical information as we move into a 5th dimensional new realm and prepare ourselves to create new socio-economic systems and potentials. They offer mediation and empowerment for equanimity, balance, peace, respect, and process for planets within the council to air grievances and concerns.

The Star Council resides and works within the 6th and 7th dimensional frequency and sometimes will crossover in cases like a planetary ascension. It is in the potential for Earth to become and celebrated within this council and others like it. Gaia will become the thirteenth planet within the auspices of the council.

Gratitude Affirmation

I trust all that I create, manifest, and experience and all has purpose to serve me in my expansion. I am blessed and grateful to experience this moment, for it further enmeshes me with all within Creation that I surrender into for guidance, unconditional love, and profound entanglement and belonging.

As often as possible, create affirmations and recite them knowing that your voice activates the cellular and innate to work in cohesive union to manifest the desires you intend. There is nothing you cannot create providing you imbue your imagination with pure intent and love. You are at the core and centre of magical energetic deliverance; create your life to be so. These simple yet powerful tasks alter and shift your life in profound ways from being a bystander to an active participant and creative master. Being in a state of gratitude will allow you to remain an active participant of all the experiences that unfold.

Alignment Exercise

Visualize that you are in a place of rest, comfort, or peaceful place. Tune into the sounds, the smells, and the sensations of all that envelopes you. Allow yourself to feel your connection with all that is alive around you and feel yourself, your innate cellular structure, and your energetic consciousness, all that you are, seeping into and floating within the environment that you are entangled with.

Like liquid light, Source, the nutrients that flow to all corners of the cosmos, are in every speck of every molecule and cell that you expanding yourself to. Visualize the golden white liquid light of Source cleansing and expanding you, soothing, and renewing you. You become one with Source, the Universe, Creation, and imagine yourself flowing with it as it moves ever farther into the cosmos and back to Earth. This is how fluid you are as spirit essence.

This visualization is key and can be done with anything that creates a thrill within your core. This process of imbuing and enmeshing yourself within all that surrounds you assists in the natural link, integration, and connection that we will require as we move into our 5th dimensional realm. Expanding yourself to be one with All That Is, and swimming with playful abandon with all that exists around us, can allow us to see, feel, hear, touch, smell, and experience life and love in a whole new way.

This expansive and integrative sensate paradigm that we as a collective have missed for so very long is the key to living a more intimate and meaningful life. We are awakening the importance of reconnecting, re-linking, reengaging, and enmeshing ourselves once again with the greater aspects of the benevolence in which we have always existed within. The desire for intimate knowledge, intimate existence, and intimate cohesion with all else within Creation is the missing link and one we are igniting within us now.

Chapter XI

First Contact

In 2012, the prohibition for interstellar contact was lifted and those who feel ready, prepared, and excited to do so, can expand what they believe to be true and create potentials for greater communion and contact with our celestial family and friends. Never before has there been the opportunity to expand our vibrational frequency for the safe and profound experience of first contact to occur.

Once we choose to create whatever it is we desire and expand our potential to experience the cosmos in a grander way we will enter the exciting and intriguing path work toward ascension. It is not possible to live in limitation, doubt, fear, and expect to meet higher vibrational beings as these two frequencies and states of being do not attract one another. So even though the quarantine is over and other beings are now assisting Earth, we must exercise our freewill and act to evolve into a being that can interact with those beings who are within the celestial lightships.

Since my awakening, I have come to know my guides. Remember, we are multi-dimensional beings and can create the illusion of physically being here, while also being on a myriad of other levels, realms, and experiences simultaneously. The more expanded we allow ourselves to become, the more awakened we allow ourselves to be, the more energetic bleed-through will occur for us to learn from, delight in, and expand upon.

Some of my visitation experiences have taken place on ships, and even other planets, so I have done my best to colour the picture for you so that you too can experience the beauty and unique elegance of what awakening into our full human potential can offer. Allow these offerings to inspire you and allow you to tap into the possibility of what is a potential should you continue on your path to ascension.

Feelings about First Contact

As we approach first contact, we will need to release our limiting beliefs about the cosmos and our world so that we can align with higher and more unlimited potential and see our reality with fresh eyes. As we draw ever closer to open contact, we need to explore the concepts, fears, and beliefs that are keeping us from evolving.

Experiences like the Roswell Incident allow us the opportunity to further refine how we feel about such cosmic experiences. If we experience an emotional reaction when we hear these stories, it is an opportunity to reflect. Perhaps your response is the perfectly timed trigger based on your life blue print to explore these emotions and feelings and gain growth and understanding and move beyond the belief system that is holding you back.

In order to create self-clarity, we must seek answers from within, and these practices will assist in the preparation for a powerfully infinite 5th dimensional life. The expanded thought results from reflection directly affects our level of consciousness and, by extension, or core vibrational state. Ask yourself the following questions. Are these feelings about ascension and first contact bringing on excitement or fear, and why? What are my beliefs that are holding me in 3D? What are my underlying perceptions and notions about my safety, and my earthly experience about my soul blueprint? Do I trust what is unfolding for me? What part about this concept excites me? Can I further act on this excitement to open and allow my path to unfold in ways that are more miraculous?

How we feel and how we perceive evolutionary expanding events, such as UFO sightings, alien contact, and the experiences known as abductions or visitations, can reveal how our current level of consciousness is limiting us and what we need to do to prepare for actual encounters.

To alter our own consciousness and create the resonance at which we can commune with higher vibrational beings, we must first uncover and examine our feelings and beliefs about how other beings may look and act. Reflection is the most effective tool for finding and addressing our deep seeded beliefs that are limiting our progress.

First contact is a natural, beautiful, enlightening, and profound aspect of planetary evolution. It is vital that we face and own all of our outdated three-dimensional beliefs, attitudes, and perceptions about who we are, and our place within the infinite Universe and the myriad of beings that inhabit it.

Go within and seek the answers to your discomfort and fear. Commune with your guides and your Higher Self, and integrate the lessons from the challenges that arise. This process allows for vibration realignment and refinement. As we expand in our awareness, we understand again that we all knew what we were doing when our blueprint was drawn up. It is with this profound recognition and acknowledgement that we can begin to transform limitation into power.

I am passionate about delivering this and many other creative works that tie in the expansive aspect of Universal energy, ascension, and how we are intimately involved in this planetary evolution as a united family and will eventually lead to open contact with our celestial families. I have seen a great gap between the understanding of spirituality and why first contact occurs. There are seemingly two trains of thoughts in these areas; Lightship or UFO sightings, and Ascension and/or enlightenment work. We're not yet seeing a marriage of these excitements and aspects of planetary and human evolution, which seem to be inherently entangled. You cannot have one without the other and both aspects are enmeshed within one another. We are, as a human race, understanding in our awakening that the marriage of our human body, with the Divine spiritual body that we have all been gifted with, is key, and is crucial if we desire to move beyond the limitation that has held in stagnancy for so long.

To create the essence of ascension is to understand that life and this experience is so much grander than we ever thought. Not only will we open ourselves up to the magical ways that Universal energy works within existence itself, but also we will tap into our infinite potential to create, manifest, and design a more powerful and enlightening life and everything we touch. As we do so, as we live with powerful intent and follow our passion, we open the energetic doorway for others within our Universe of like vibration to reach out and assist us on our path of growing awareness. This is why we're seeing a profound increase in experiences involving lightships, extra-terrestrials, and UFOs. Every time we engage with the cosmos with wonderment, expanded thought, and leading edge discussions about human potential, we are offering a welcome mat to those who also desire connection and entanglement at a more conscious and open manner.

As all things exist as one, we cannot look at only one aspect of Creation and ignore all others. As we better understand our expanding states of potential, we also understand the need for truthful, respectful dialogue about what contact entails. How will we open ourselves to these potentials in our everyday lives?

The potential to create greater Universal Unity is within every thought, word, and deed that we imbue with love and open-minded intent. Our desire for engagement at a much higher frequency, and a much deeper and more intimate level will ignite us and propel us into an ascended status. Intimacy and entanglement stirs the soul to manifest experiences for us to awaken into our infinite profundity and connect with the myriad of celestials and high order councils that hover in the night sky and they celebrate every step we make to create such potentials for humanity and Creation. As we expand, we understand more each day the potential that has been untapped for aeons and once again, we can look to the skies with fresh loving eyes and celebrate our place among the cosmos with our celestial family.

In our remembrances, as we awaken, we delight in the exploration and desire to seek a greater blending of science and the unseen, for it is existence itself. We will see our societal structures take more expansive approaches in aligning with people's desire for harmony, enlightened living, and co-existing in exciting and energetic ways without the care or worry of what others say or do. We will expand into states of joy and bliss, and gather in great numbers to inspire and empower a natural and more unified approach to all that we touch.

As we intend to experience and see only the good in everything, we will create the holographic reality that equally matches these powerful intentions. These are vibrations of our New 5th dimensional Earth and the illuminated galactic human that we co-create in these enlightened behaviours. We will remember why we are here playing this magnificent game, and finally unite as we build the infinite bridge to our glowing Universal home.

Evolution is upon us and that means our expansive understanding about multi-dimensional beings, our relationship with them, and our existing in harmony will be the exciting role we will play over the coming years to move us further in our growth as an ascended planet.

Letting Go of Fear

These experiences are not to be feared even though they feel unusual, strange, or weird, but we must stretch beyond our limitations and try to remember that we already know these visitors. We *are* these beings, they are an aspect of us and they are all reaching out their hands to assist us in our evolutionary process.

It is not always easy. More than once, I have popped out of a meditative state when overwhelmed by the unfamiliarity of a new being that is attempting to link with me. It is important to realize that these species are quite advanced and they have been operating as advanced civilizations for a long time and if we give it a chance, we will soon get used to the insectoids, reptilian-hybrids, felines, and bird people.

The more I work on my inner beliefs, the more available I am to open to the vibration of otherworldly beings without fear and judgement. This is why our multi-dimensional family and friends come to us in dreams and meditations, so that they can ease us into the experience.

All of the beings connecting and linking with us are doing so because we have aligned ourselves to their vibration as we work through our soul blueprint. We already have contracts and agreements with these beings that are connecting with us once we reach a higher state of awareness. Our Higher Self will align with these beings when the timing is right according to our won preordained plans.

As we reach a level of refinement that will allow these amazing experiences to occur without a hindrance to our current physical life, we will move into the flow of contact. These multi-dimensional experiences are the merging and the braiding of our higher aspects with our Earth consciousness and it is a powerful demarcation that you have ascended to such a level for this to occur.

The Right Frequency

One aspect of planetary ascension is to prepare us to interact with our greater cosmic family. Our greater cosmic family resonates at much higher frequencies than we do at the moment, but the ascension process that humanity is experiencing will allow those who so desire the opportunity to expand in vibration to match the level in which contact may be possible.

Now that we know we are multi-dimensional spirit essence, we can conjure the myriad of levels that we must integrate and expand into in order to match a higher state. The ability to meet higher resonant beings with success and safety for all requires many years of preparation and integration has been designed at every level. It would be non-beneficial if we were to glitch under the difference in resonance, and spew ourselves in a downward spiral as we face the profound purity of their essence.

When beings of a higher state meet with us, we must be ready and aligned energetically. There must be a vibrational match for these events to occur safely. Those beings in a higher resonate states would jeopardize their vibrational state and we could be prone to psychic or energetic shock if we were operating on vastly different resonances.

Gaia's evolution is not a whimsical musing. There are teams of beings throughout Creation who are observing and assisting with initiation activations of individuals to support the Divine plan for Gaia's ascension and they are assisting us in developing the appropriate higher-level frequencies.

As we move closer to first contact, we will experience higher levels of, and more refined types of, energy to further stretch who and what we are. Everything in our reality is being altered and our whole aspect is shifting to keep up as we adjust to these energetic recalibration into a 5th dimensional frequency.

We should ask ourselves what aspects of our current reality keep us from moving forward and expanding into greater spiritual awareness and reconnecting with Creation, and the many illuminated beings that also desire to reunite in a loving manner.

Planetary ascension is the process of shifting our state of consciousness to integrate an expanded understanding and providing us with the capacity to resonate at a frequency that will enable us to commune with beings who have already ascended. This profound trans-formative process will also allow us to feel freer, lighter, and faster.

One must experience one level of existence and consciously create the opportunities and resonance that shift them to a new and improved experience. To do so, one must tap into the self-discovery process to reveal the unconditional offerings of love, patience, reverence, support, and commitment that we are always being given. The soul's desire for entanglement with Source, Creation, and one another is the loving catalyst that creates the expansive experiences. Ascension really can feel like a loving spiral that brings about change in every way possible and all rotating and circling around the Central Source of this Universe.

Choose Brilliance

The frequency in which we resonate directly affects the potential outcomes. Even in a random situation can manifest the best outcome if we resonate at a high enough frequency. Define it so, align to it, and so it shall be. Perceiving one's environment is not created on the outside, it is created from within first. This is how profound of a creator we truly are. We create our perceptions from within from what we believe to be true and how we define it to be so. Define brilliance in all that encompasses your life, and so it shall be. What we perceive is not defined by outside powers, but everything is created within each of us. We create our perceptions based on our beliefs. So, if we commit to defining everything I our lives in brilliance, so it shall be.

Everything in existence has a vibrational frequency, and it is a process of dialling into the frequency that will best serve you on your chosen path. The words that you use, the beliefs that you imbue yourself with, will ultimately create the reality you experience. Be aware of how you think, what you say, and alter it in the moment to serve your needs. It may appear like a massive amount of effort, but once you have programmed your system with new beliefs, new profound definitions, and altered your state of thinking, it will flow as naturally as breathing.

When alignment is natural and fluid your systems will seek out and intuitively know the best frequency. This is mastery. Now that you know this, you can create the life you truly desire by reflecting upon what beliefs serve and propel you in a profound way, and then choose definitions in each moment to align with heightened beliefs that support the frequency shift. What you think, what you believe, what you emit will create and manifest your entire reality. Your world will change when you change, and it all starts within. When you are aware, and expand your consciousness to heightened states and profound vibrations, you then shift all other outcomes to create a more profound potential. This is how magical you are and how profound this experience can be for those that tap into the infinite potentials in awareness, consciousness, and the refinement process. We create our own version of Heaven on Earth within ourselves and it starts now.

You can choose to move down new, exciting paths of enlightenment regarding all aspects of your life, or you can choose to remain unchanged. You can choose active participation in creating a magnificent life, or you can choose to remain right where you are. You are in complete control so create a healthier, more peaceful, loving, intimate, and healthy worldly experience.

Cosmic Visitations

We have a myriad of skilled and brilliant celestials and guides who will deliver experiences and lessons as we gain insight, and expand into heightened awareness. Until we are ready, many of the multi-dimensional memories or experiences will, at first, be delivered in our dreams or meditations and as we explore the deeper meaning of these messages, the dreams, impressions, and visitations will flow more readily as our energy signature is cleared of the blockages causes by fear and negativity.

These experiential triggers are a trait of the initiation, of ascension, and awakening. When you realize there are infinite realms within existence, or higher frequencies, expanded awareness, open and unlimited potential in thought and acceptance, then you can truly understand that you that you have potential to manifest within this.

We cannot perceive what we are not the vibration of. Soon you will know, without question, that you have become a master creator and that you are being prepared for the eventuality of first contact and first landings as we co-create the new Earth.

Those who have consciously chosen ascension will have in some way experienced an aspect of cosmic visitation. These experiences will have come in dreams, impressions during meditation, or even a physical contact. Although, often, we are made to forget the experience until we have achieved the vibration where these instances can be remembered, integrated, and understood in the grander plan of who we are and what we are entangled within. We are carefully being shown, in many ways, that our reach is much farther than we ever thought possible.

Other realm experiences or sensing will also be activated much more frequently as more people are triggered into the awakening phase. As we unfurl into our higher states of being, we accept, embrace, and practice further expansion techniques because we feel like we finally fit within our expanding reality and our reality is mirroring back to us the magical transformation that we exhibit.

I have always had an amazing team of celestial and extra-terrestrial beings assisting me in every step of my life process. Their presence in my life has helped me overcome depression and suicide, as well as guiding me away from paths that would have led to a negative and drastic outcome for me. We are always loved, supported, and unconditionally guided toward our higher light.

My understandings and remembrance of my intimate connections with those in other star systems have become some of my most valued and treasured gifts in this entire ascension process. To feel the depth of unconditional love at this planetary level is humbling and transformative. This is a process that we are moving toward, and I feel great excitement as I pass along the wisdom and information I gain from these multi-dimensional experiences to all those who attract themselves to it. I believe the discovery of unconditional love, and the discovery of our infinite potential are just some of the primary remembrances that we are exposing to ourselves with each passing revelation and it is why so many of us volunteered for this powerful incarnation. There are few planetary realms that offer the lessons that we are offered in this earthly experience, so celebrate your existence in this fact alone.

The Universe is vast and multi-layered and it is a reflection of our own multi-layered aspects. At the highest vibrational level of the One, and then All That Is, all the way down to over soul family groups, the over soul, the individual soul, the Higher Self, the spirit self, and physical self, we have all of these aspects that also mirror our other aspects that are linked and grounded at the centre of Creation. The innate journey to Source, to light, to the beginning from which we were all created, is the reason for all the lessons on every level and realm in which we experience. By expanding our awareness and consciousness, we gain greater understanding for All That Is and it is in this over-riding desire to embrace our wholeness that we come to tread some of the most profound courses and lifetimes. In this earthly incarnation, if we choose to recognize and integrate any form of light and love, we will transform the entire human species. The potential to meet with inter-stellar beings in our meditations and dreams and be conscious enough to recreate and refine these processes until we are of a vibration that allows us the intelligence and awareness to cosmically travel anywhere we desire is infinite and amazing.

Chapter XII

Multi-Dimensional Contact

Preparation for Contact

My insatiable curiosity has been with me my entire life. Curiosity is a key attribute to ascension as it is the catalyst that drives us to continue seeking.

I remember. as a child, we would often have summertime sleepovers, laying under a brilliant night sky on our patio and I would ponder at the enormity of the space that seemed to cradle us. I would wonder about the possibilities of meeting intelligent beings from our neighbouring planets. What would they look like? What could they teach us? How big is our Universe, and will we create the necessary technology so that, one day, I could explore the Universe? More and more people now are awakening to these very questions.

Lightship sightings inspire honest dialogue about how we feel about our celestial neighbours and family, as well as our ability to step up into the vibration where open contact is possible. Higher dimensional beings resonate at a rate much higher and faster than we do, and we must be prepared for this very real experience that will be sensed in every way when contact occurs. Our energetic resonance will be affected, our physical body will be affected, and we need to bring our frequency up to a level where safe and loving contact can be made without the repercussions of such energetic differences.

Until we are used to seeing and interacting with beings that look nothing like us, we will need to co-create experiences that can ease us into awareness at a pace that is safe and empowering for us. In meditations, dreams, and impressions we are introduced to many of our energetic and celestial team members who are assisting and guiding us. We may not always know whether these beings that we meet in our heightened states of awareness are on our team or would alternate aspects of ourselves. We do not need to know the details of their place of origin, or their name, or even why they were assigned to us. What is important, in these multi-dimensional experiences, is that we take the symbols and lessons offered and reflect upon what we can learn in this moment of now.

There will be challenges and some of these challenges will feel overwhelming. Know that it is not necessary to control every element of a profound multi-dimensional download or experience. We are given these meetings, these contacts, in a manner that will allow us to take what is important for us to know and to absorb it, relish within it, and alter who we are because of it. To make these experiences easier for our consciousness to open up, these beings will cloak themselves with loving feelings and gentle memories in order to appear non-threatening and plausible. Our guides are committed to allowing us the opportunity to remain in a heightened state in order to experience these communications, lessons, or gifts.

They do this by attempting to look as familiar as possible. I have had many interactions with many beings and each time something was slightly odd or different about their physical appearance. It may have been their height, hands, or legs, or shape of their body. In my waking conscious state, I often pondered these experiences. Often the difference in their physical appearance was part of the symbolism of their message. Remember, there are no boundaries to thought projection and energetic transference of data and information.

I have insectoids and reptilian-humanoids within my soul family, and they often check-in with me through my dreams and meditations. But when they first entered my awareness they cloaked themselves in aspects that I would recognize and understand, allowing these experiences to unfold without fear. Their appearance is becoming more natural as I open my awareness and become familiar with their resonance and physicality. I have had dreams and meditations with many varied humanoid beings and I know at some level these quasi-humanoid beings will project or cloak themselves in a way through each progressive interaction that will match my awareness, readiness, and resonance. I am slowly familiarizing and remembering the work that we do in other realms and star systems.

These multi-dimensional visitations are necessary to prepare us and guide us as we learn to stretch our consciousness to enable us to receive the insight and intuitive data to facilitate our expansion and ascension. Beings from all over the Universe have the ability to insert themselves into our heightened states of consciousness, to fulfil the plans in our soul blueprints, as well as the cosmic agenda for our ascension and evolution.

Multi-dimensional insertions occur slowly and have been seeping into our consciousness for a long time now. All of these preparations allow us to partake in the potential for a greater diversity, expanded understandings, loving celestial connections, and the comprehension of the concepts that will enable the grounding of future Earth, the future illuminated human, and a new 5th dimensional planet that will be unified within the cosmos. We are evolving in each moment when we allow ourselves to open up to a broader point of view of who we are and what our ultimate potential is. We are creating a bridge for communications, agreement, and strengthened galactic bodies where we all serve one another in light, in love, and in Divine benevolence that mirrors Source and the code of Creation.

The most profound lesson I have learned, however, is despite the physical differences, we are all interwoven within Creation. Like the threads of a cosmic quilt, we carry a myriad of colours, textures, and glyphs that resonate with the personal and unique story of who we are and who we have been created to be.

Within every heartbeat, within every breath, we are the multi-coloured threads that bind the beauty of the cosmos together as one beautiful Universal blanket that spans within every cell throughout Creation. Earth is now ready to know this and expand upon it. It is our turn to join our Universal family in a much grander way. The more we open up to a greater understanding of who we are and what our role is within this grander Universal aspect of Creation, the greater connection and link we have and more intricately woven we enmesh within this quilt of infinite love and light. We open the door to these multi-dimensional insertions and communications as we work through and shed the old world limitations, outdated beliefs, and prepare our hearts to allow love at the greater Universal level. Expansion is about gaining a greater and broader view, inclusivity, and acceptance of the all.

Acceptance is key in the process of ascension for it requires that we create a level of love for thyself that humanity has never experienced before. We are ready. For if we truly explore and imbue the love for self as higher realm beings do, we then open to the profoundly endless and unconditional love that Source has for each and every one of us. It is in this sharing of our potential, our own love that we shine with the brilliance of the illuminated galactic human upon new Earth. Can we alter our beliefs and judgements about our neighbouring countries, or even next door, and build the bridge to another star system with the potential to mend the tattered blanket that spans the galaxy?

Physical Evolution

We have within us the power to activate our cellular structure so that we can align the chemical mechanisms, which can heal and propel any aspect within our physical body. The ability to increase our metabolism, to heal wounds or illness, and even extend or reverse time is available to those in heightened states of awareness. We need to align ourselves with an intentional state to commune with all aspects of who we are, what we are entangled with, and create an appropriate level of self-love and self-interest to bring in the changes needed for healing. This is how profoundly powerful we are in that we can direct and intend the life we desire in every way. When we hear about miraculous reports of people who have spontaneously healed themselves, know they have all of these links in the glorious chain of Creation working in alignment for their perfect health.

The power we have within to instruct our innate aspects,

the cellular aspects, and the teams we have supporting us to all join in the process of healing, rejuvenation, and propulsion into higher frequencies is not only possible, but what most higher realm beings operate on as a natural attribute of their existence.

It is in these teachings, in these experiences, every new concept we allow to seep into our consciousness is a potential for us to explore that literally changes the speed at which we resonate. Our chemical constituents are being shifted to trigger our awakening and ascension. Even as you read this, you may become triggered, for in every word there is resonance and ancient wisdom that is flowing from me to you for remembrance and activation.

Your team and spirit guides will inspire you and they will send you clues (like this book) to bring you to new level of awareness so you can realign with your profoundly Divine self. When the love of the Divine reaches out, your physical body will react. You may experience goose bumps, chills, or the feeling of familiarity to information even though it is new to your consciousness. This is your physical body's way of alerting you to the moment, the vibration of your own Divine profundity. You have been mirrored the exact potential of what you are capable of creating for yourself and a part of your greater self knows this. At the very core of who we are, there is pure Divine love and as love is the most powerful frequency within our Universe, it will affect us in every aspect of our being.

As we acknowledge and declare who we are with clear, positive, and powerful new beliefs and unlimited expansive potential, the path to the infinite begins and the portals to Universal wisdom and innate abilities will open, initiating the transformation of our physical bodies. Every aspect of who we are is constantly engaged at the energetic level with all that we exist within. This level of self-clarity and declaration will activate cell efficiency, maximize health, and even create a youthful looking body, for we own the potential to steer our life experience in this way. The more aware we are of these human potentials, the more we can carve a path to what we truly desire. As our cells speed up, our thinking will accelerate and our experiences will align with our ever-refined state. We will be able to do more in less time, because we are coalescing with our environment with energetic cohesion and profundity. We have been conditioned to believe that we have little control over our bodies and our environment and that's why we believe our health rests in the hands of the pharmaceutical companies to maintain our lifespan.

Symptoms of Ascension

Our species is moving through an energetic first in respect to the level of transformation. It really is quite a mystery as to exactly how and what will be forthcoming. We know that we are shifting, changing, and altering not only our etheric bodies, but also our physical bodies. With more intensified planetary shifts, it can seem as if our bodies are playing catch up with what is swirling around us. The physicality of who we are is also transforming, as we're becoming more and more refined as we continue to expand into our higher celestial selves.

In this time of fine-tuning and refinement, we are experiencing increased sensitivity as we connect more deeply with the energy fields of the planet. We are being given opportunities to recognize what needs to be honoured and healed within, which will allow us to move on into higher vibrational levels. This is the stage of not only awakening, but of refinement. Our body and all aspects of who we are will be affected and as Gaia shifts, so will we. All of these profound energetic changes are to prepare us for open conscious contact and to be able to sustain ourselves within a highly refined 5th dimensional realm.

As I move through my process of ascension, there are days where I feel as if I'm in my fifth and even sixth dimensional energetic self and it is jostling to fit within the world around me. The subtlety of these transitions feel very real and all appears to be slightly different than the day before. I feel that if I were not grounded and aware of this process then I could literally pop out of my skin, for the speed at which I feel I am moving is faster than those around me. There are also days when my body processes so much energy that I just want to lie down for a few hours.

Our body is the temple to which all 5th dimensional change is channelled through, so it will be affected in a myriad of ways. My energy gets so intense sometimes that I literally have to focus and ground several times a day just so I can complete my daily activities.

Mastering these energetic shifts does require one to tune in to our bodies and be aware of what is happening energetically as we are all connected and enmeshed in this process. Communicating daily with our teams will also help us prepare and move through intense ascension energies because they are preparing us from a grander perspective for what is to come. There are a few simple and needed things for your temple to filter, process, and integrate the coming ascension energies for heightened manifestations and centeredness. Rest, breath work, water, grounding, and interacting with Gaia, will do wonders for rebalancing our bodies and remaining calm in times of great change.

We will develop a sense of inner knowingness so that we can gauge and understand what we are moving through and what may need further clearing energetically. We will feel as if we are highly charged as our sensitivity increases and we will feel a heightened awareness of all things around us. As we become more awakened to the feeling aspects of our being, we will recognize deeper emotions with our loved ones. Feeling immense joy and unconditional love will bring about new ways for us to create higher unity consciousness with those around us. All of these transformations will invite us to also act in loving ways, to the world around us.

Great joy will be unveiled in these times of transition, for this is the time for new beginnings and new awakenings on all levels. There is a balancing act taking place as we work more fully from our energetic self so we can feel more natural in these states and understand what these symptoms mean. At every stage of ascension, there will be different symptoms and changes. Symptoms can range from tingling sensations as our cells and chakra centres speed up, feelings of head pressure and headaches, tingling or vibrations at the base of the neck, vision and auditory sensitivity, eating and sleeping habit changes, and many more.

The important thing to remember is that everything exists at the energy level first. Whether the manifestation is illness, ascending limitation, or first contact, all change occurs because we have at some level created the energy for it to appear to us in the experiential way. The more in-tune we are to our body and our environment, the more adept we will become at sensing the path before us. It is always important to check with our medical professional in any area that causes you concern. If we approach all transformations with excitement and joy, then any symptoms will subside as love soothes and heals at the deepest level.

The Ascension Master

I am blessed to feel my way through this experience now as opposed to going through the motions and over-thinking everything. Mastery is the ability to not only design and create the physical path by aligning and shifting our inner vibration, but to also master how we go about experiencing the path. If we are using the tools we have been given by the Creator, and we awaken to what lies beyond what we can see, we will find the power, the will, the intent, and all other aspects we want to use, within ourselves.

We can master our vibration to the point where each and every situation is reflected and altered to match our path, and our path is ever changing, because we are. We are flowing with the vibrations and synchronicities as they unfold because we have practiced our communication with our teams, we discern the symbolism that fits our style, and we trust all that is blossoming because we know, in some way, that it serves us. The master within us all resides at the core of our being. It is the encoded Divine essence and the all-knowing guide that sees the entire scope of Creation and how we fit within it all. Allowing the master to awaken

255

within us is to acknowledge and declare to the Universe, to Source, to our guides, and our celestial team that we are engaged, we are all knowing, and we desire guidance as unveil our profound potential.

Waking up within this amazing game of experiential reality is why many are tuning in and aligning with a 5th dimensional vibration. Innately deep within us all, we have the vibrational patterns to adapt to any vibration we choose. We are now awakening to the master within us that can coach us and align us to the channel we desire. As we become faster and higher vibrating beings, we physically become lighter and thus open up to be more receptive to refined and accelerated frequencies and downloads so our expanding path can continue. Ever upward, ever onward, we travel in oneness, in celestial companionship, and in light and love for all because we know we are within this all.

The higher aspect of who we are becomes visible as we craft our lives with knowingness in our own profundity, and the master awakens within. A master knows that all is linked, entangled, and connected, and to be One with this, and walk in our own unique way, is the desire of light workers— to coalesce with the infinite quantum energetic realm in which we float. This is the understanding, the awakening of our master potential to create our lives with clarity, with purpose, with resolve to be the creator and the driver in this profound physical experience. The awakening to ascension is unique, special, infinite, and magical to each person. If only my lessons and my stories of experience can shed even the slightest light on something this profound, then the vast array of potential that awaits each person can be seen with less fear, less doubt, and greater excitement that lies beyond the veil of limitation.

Our Multi-Dimensional Family

When we better understand the realm of energetic patterning that we live within and dance within, we can create and master our behaviour and energy in a new and profound way. Understanding our infinite and multi-dimensional potential allows us to expand upon what we know to be true about not only the heritage of humanity, but the potential of our parallel aspects and the ancient ones hovering in the sky — waiting for us to awaken to this. As we expand upon the understanding of Universal energy in all of its glory and form, there is not one aspect of life, as we know it that is not touched.

Our multi-dimensional family exists as an arm, a branch, a flower, a leaf from the greater tree of life that we are connected to. Just like our neighbours in the most war-torn countries, we ingest the same nutrients from Source that all of life does. Somehow, at some point, we forgot that link which exists within us all, but our loving multi-dimensional family has arrived and now we have the opportunity to acknowledge and embrace the life that beats within us all with their guidance and assistance.

I am most passionate about our multi-dimensional families. Over the past few years, I have had the opportunity to share things I have learned about the multiple versions of me and my experiences with so many multi-dimensional beings. Some of these beings have taken on a physical form and some have not during their interactions with me. Some beings have shown me that they have the ability to shift their shape or at least cloak themselves in a different form. They have done this to ease me into a state where I can safely or comfortably interact with them and learn from them. They are committed to helping us overcome our conditioning that makes us afraid or judgemental about them.

As our collective consciousness has inspired mass awakenings, there will be countless new discoveries, experiences, and contacts with other life forms, thus propelling us further along a path of human evolution that is beyond anything experienced before on Earth.

Our celestial family and friends exist in a myriad of forms and in a vast number of consciousness levels. Our role is to expand our consciousness state to the point where we are comfortable, accepting, and loving of all beings on all planets. Some multi-dimensional beings have forms that are similar to that of ours, humanoid, and some are completely different.

We have always been guided and visited by our extended family and other beings from other planets. Many of our spirit guides are celestial beings that we have worked with as they were assigned to us from realms that we may have already visited in other lifetimes. In ancient cultures there was a greater understanding and connection between our celestial family members than we have now. Our multi-dimensional family has many roles, most essentially to impart wisdom as we expand and prepare for contact.

Visitation is not new and it is not for the purpose of an alien race coming to take over our planet or to enslave humanity. Visitation is for the purpose of growth and expansion between all parties and the Universe, Source, and existence as a whole.

Our growing and expanding awareness will create infinite potential for all beings and it is what will create the glow of new Earth. It is the vibration of trust, love, and allowance that we belong to a family much more expansive and diverse than we could ever have dreamt. This expanding awareness and awakening for humanity will create reverberations of energetic waves that literally shift how we behave, how we manifest, and how we move about our lives. The gates of acceptance, to who we truly are and what our potential may be, will swing open.

As we truly open to all of these grander perspectives of our multi-dimensional family and our placement within the immensity of it all, we can then welcome the benevolent beings that stretch across the Universe resulting in a united heart within the Divine.

For me, it was only a matter of ten years in which I moved from a state of semi-awareness to my current state of preparation for contact with light and higher realm beings. I started this path with excitement, spurred on by a spiritual revelation that came during a meditative experience that literally changed everything in my life. The resonance of that spiritual trigger, that Divine moment that changed me as it touched my heart, ignited my soul into a state of love and remembrance, which propelled me into seeking more. When awakening and remembrance hit me, I knew and it was like falling in love for the first time. It occupied my every thought, my every moment.

As I have been gifted to awaken on this path, I see and understand the state of remembrance that we as a collective sit in now and I am inspired to offer what insights I can for the potential of unbelievable possibilities for all of humanity. To relearn the wisdom of the indigenous peoples, the shamanic ones that linked their energetic thread with those in the sky, I am inspired to walk forward with passion and reflection for a world in which my children will not know war or struggling to survive. This is our potential and our multi-dimensional family are ushering us through a gateway to new Earth.

Multi-Dimensional Communication

As we activate, we will begin to notice that our dreams and meditative experiences will start to take on new meanings. This process opens the portals that will enable us to expand to enable a connection with our multi-dimensional family, which will ultimately allow us to consciously meet. Knowing how to communicate at a multi-dimensional consciousness level is key and it is not all that difficult.

Ascension is a process of being in a state of continual movement, growth, and ascending vibrations. This evolution will enable us to meet our celestial family.

Our daily experiences should take on a heightened vibration that resonates at the frequency of our multi-dimensional associates and the incremental work we are doing will facilitate a steady adaptation to the appropriate ascendant frequencies. Eventually you will be introduced to a myriad of beings and other aspects of *you* that exists in other planetary realms.

Communication is usually initiated in dreams, meditations, and higher states of consciousness where we are given creative free reign to be as close to our spirit self as possible. Multi-dimensional communication is opened up by our readiness and purity of intent to move into new levels of heightened awareness.

Our teams will design and align experiences for us in a myriad of ways to give us ample opportunity to step up our vibrations and expand our awareness. Our role is to release limiting beliefs, align with our highest state, ask with the purity of intent, and allow. Trust what unfolds to you. Ultimately, the catalyst to any ascension path is our ability to act.

Opening up to multi-dimensional communication is our destiny, but we must first commit to acting in alignment with those that place benevolence above all. It is vital that we take the time to reflect upon how these unfolding multi-dimensional communication subtleties that are found in every symbol, concept, vision, impression, or dreamlike experience are serving us in the Now. I have learned over the many years of honing my communication skills, with various beings, that the message is incredibly subtle. It will take some effort on our part not to miss the cues and gifts offered to us. We assume it should resonate like everything else in our world; loud, noisy, and blatant, but that is rarely the case.

Retire to your quiet reflective state, ground your vessel to Gaia, and ask with a purity of heart for the intention to link and communicate with members of your team and you will be given a sign. You can then build upon these simple requests until you and your team have developed a free flowing pathway of communication that can be taken anywhere. Your team will design symbols, stories, or concepts that will meet your level of understanding and creative expression. There is nothing that is not heard, seen, or known by your team. They can see through your eyes and they will maintain a constant link and engagement with us as we flow through life.

These reflections and integrations will allow you to expand and increase your personal frequency to allow for greater multi-dimensional communication and all within Creation will benefit from your inner work. For every story, every being has its vibrational place within this immensely infinite puzzle. As each being explores their most authentic, Divine self, the puzzle becomes profoundly more complete.

Activating Multi-Dimensional Experiences

When dreams open up all sorts of new experiences and our way daily thoughts become engaged with light and the infinite potential for humanity, we will find the process of ascension has become a passion as it unveils more of who we truly are. Aligning to greater multi-dimensional experiences occurs when we surrender what was and step into what is. We *are* already multi-dimensional beings of Divine spirit essence and it is our natural evolutionary process to progress from our current state of limitation and denial about our potential and evolve into an illuminated galactic human.

Surrendering into the vibration of the Divine's depth of unconditional love and allowance for all that you are — even when you feel you are the most flawed, scarred, and undesirable person — will facilitate the beginning of a healing process in which light will penetrate even the most stubborn of your barricades.

Ascension and multi-dimensional experiences, communication, and the enhancement of our skills are generated at the heart level. All things Divine are unified in the realm of love, forgiveness, release, acceptance, self-love, self-honour, and the desire to belong — in the heart. If we set the intention to reveal and release all negative and limiting beliefs and soul scars, then ask for healing and guidance, we will receive. This work will free us and we will feel lighter as the cloudy energetic karma is released and we are healed. The declaration of intent to open up to one's full potential will create magnetic sparks of potential that will naturally align us with our profundity and allow for greater free flow of multi-dimensional gifts from our teams and the Universe, all who are collaborating for our evolution and advancement. This is how loved we are.

In order to open up to our full potential and unleash our innate power to create and link with the Universal web of infinite information and design, we must first ensure to work through old beliefs in moments of deep reflection in order to create a balance that will be the starting point for more advanced energy work and experiences.

We are stepping into unknown territory as this is a new potential for all of humanity and there are few real guidebooks. However, as we work through our issues, we will feel the new must first ensure that reflection time is being done to work through old beliefs so that true balance can be a starting point for more advanced energy work and experiences and know we are moving out from behind the veil of illusion and moving in the right direction.

When we acknowledge and own the depth of our brilliance and ability, we will be shown how to unleash the unlimited and profound energetic potential that we already hold within, as we are infinite beings of light. Then we will know our power to change the vibration of our paths in only the moment it takes to say it aloud.

Declaring your intent, your active role in the life you desire to experience is your promise to get back in the driver's seat and start carving your own path with unwavering focus. We acknowledge all that we cannot see as being alive, among us, within us, and we are merely aligning with the matching vibration for us to see it and experience it. We offer an open invitation to the myriad of beings, whose specific role is to offer Divine assistance for this very path of awakening, to guide us.

As we are offered the energetic gifts, the inspirations, the meditative and dream communications, and the synchronistic opportunities, then our role becomes to merely remain open to what may unfold. To remain open, we must allow ourselves the knowingness that we trust in all that we are a part of. Trust what comes to you in the form of symbols, circumstances, or situations. Express with every ounce of your being that you trust the process, the Divine, your guides, your team, and ultimately yourself for creating every experience at these highest of consciousness states. When you trust to the level of allowance, you begin to flow with the profound stream of electromagnetic currents that bring you to exactly where you need to be. You then only need to act upon what excites you to move you further along your path. Appreciate, validate, and trust what unfolds and you will flow with this profound stream and you will experience the most magical of results.

Navigating Multi-Dimensional Experiences

Expanding our perceptions enough to play in these energetic offerings and be in a constant state of allowance, can allow us to more easily navigate the even more intense and refined streams that will be sent. Until Gaia is in her 5th dimensional footing, we will continue to experience extremes in energetic shifting. Pulsating streams of light rays and information in various forms, all better expand those who are tapped into this process. They will also help

Gaia continue Her efforts at re-balancing. In these times of great shifts, the multi-dimensional experiences will also shift.

Some multi-dimensional beings have acquired a certain vibratory level and skill to present a version of themselves or their essence in our dreams, meditations, or heightened consciousness states. There are beings that can create cloaks in order to create impressions or feelings of a particular form when interacting with us. To navigate our way around such experiences requires knowing that we are at the centre of these magical occurrences. This will release the worry, the confusion, and the doubt about what we receive in these heightened states.

As we ascend and open to our true multi-dimensional potential, we will gain the necessary expertise to enable and facilitate our interactions with all the higher realm beings that pop in and out of our daily lives to assist, guide, and protect us. We will gain understanding about each being's style of communicating as we continue our regular practice and reflection to amp up our potential for sightings of their lightships. This process of ascension is one that gradually allows us to work our way into the energy of these experiences, but we must prepare ourselves so that they can be enjoyed, accepted, and embraced more fully.

The consciousness must be prepared to receive the multi-dimensional aspects of the information and energetic resonances that are inherent in the ascension process. Navigating our way through these experiences is key and all it really requires is quiet reflection and meditation where we request validation and confirmation from our teams and then integrating the information, wisdom, and lessons that we receive. We must also work through our negative belief patterns and redefine our lives in ways that are more powerful. It is vital that we refine our consciousness by meditating, communing with nature, and reflecting on the lessons in order to integrate them before we can expect to have out of this world contact and multi-dimensional experiences.

There really can be no expansion if we do not first acknowledge the possibilities, our worthiness, and open ourselves to the flow of Universal wisdom and energy. This is expansion. Asking, allowing, integrating, understanding, and so on is an ongoing refinement process and will always give us further opportunity to expand.

Dreams and meditation play an integral role in this process, so pay attention, and allow your dreams to guide you. Dreams are the doorway to our expanded understanding of our multi-dimensional self and the Universe that we live within. I have been on this ascension path for many years and my multi-dimensional experiences are becoming more and more exciting and surreal, and I know they are directly aligned with the vibration of my changing core resonance. As I open, awaken, and let go of all fear, doubt, and limitation, my experiences then become higher in resonance and meaning. This, too, is possible for you.

We all move fluidly within the Universal grid-lines of electromagnetic pulls, which are the result of energetic inspirations. We move and shift so seamlessly within this infinitely layered multi-verse, and we are only just tapping into how infinite our existence truly is. As we shift, dream, or meditate we allow our consciousness to raise to the level of higher realm beings. Because we are infinite, we are simultaneously working on many levels in many realms and thus we tap into these experiences when we need to pull in a symbol or lesson where we are in our now moment.

Divine Light Being Affirmation

I am worthy, as a Divine light being, to connect with my highest purpose, my blueprint, my magnetic path and to unfold these magical experiences to me as I reengage with my team, Source, Gaia, and Creation to unfold on this path of ascension. I declare my participation and intent to live to my highest level in this physical experience, and so I ask for your guidance, love, and support in this healing transformation.

The acknowledgement and declaration of my intent to engage in this magical game is what has taken me into experiences of high-level multi-dimensional vibrations. We literally amp-up our core frequencies to match a 5th dimensional frequency.

Celebrate your life, your potential, the purpose for your existence, in the same manner that the billions of beings supporting us now do. The Universe will respond to the exact level of intent and acknowledgement that you declare yourself to yourself, to the new reality we are co-creating, to Source, and to life once again. If you declare your purpose to be that of a visitor or spectator, then that is the vibration you set and that will be exactly what you experience. Should you desire deep and profound change and potential that unfolds in all areas of your life, or even greater intimacy with the Universe and those around you, or enhanced multi-dimensional experiences, then a declaration of this vibration will bring it to you. Once you reach this level, you will be equally matching the passion that the Divine has for you and your potential.

The path of ascension teaches and expands who we are in the deepest of ways and it is this level of understanding that can adjust your path from one that is a struggle to survive, to one that is flowing with your highest potential. Clear your beliefs, redefine your life as it unfolds, anticipate success, and love at every step. Acknowledge your worthiness to live in the vibration of light and the multi-dimensional brilliance that resides within you to create. Declare your intent to the Universe, for the belief in your own worthiness propels you and your desire to live a more finely tuned and connected life with all that is around you. As your path unfolds, amps up, and brings magical opportunities to you, you can then practice reflecting upon the symbolism, the energetic stories, and will allow the pieces of your energetic puzzle, the soul story that you designed for yourself in this life, to unfold with precision and elegance. You are truly worthy of this knowingness, so embrace and celebrate who you are in every moment, for Source and all of Creation knows this for you.

Chapter XIII

Personal Experience

Psychic Intuition

When I was a child, I had an inner knowingness or ability to sense the energies of those around me. Though confusing most of the time, I sensed that I was different. I know now that we are all born with intuitive and psychic abilities that make up the multi-dimensional aspects of who we are. More often than not, most children born into such gifted sensitivities become numb to their gifts as they are conditioned into our physically dense world.

I could tune into someone and sense a great deal about them, but often these people would act completely differently on the outside. That was very confusing for me, as a child, so I spent a lot of time alone, in my own head, daydreaming, writing stories, or journaling. This was my only release of the profound energy that filled me. Thankfully, my parents encouraged my creativity and writing afforded me a safe channel for the intense energetic abilities that often left me feeling quite helpless and alone.

Wherever I could find solace and peace within my own thoughts was the place I found most enjoyable. Today, children are encouraged to explore their intuitive abilities by meditating and discussing the outcomes of those mediations or their dreams, and many are awakening in the higher conscious states.

I remember, many childhood mornings, waking up with visions of other realities, other worldly beings, and experiences that seemed so real that the experiences imprinted firmly within my conscious memory. Sometimes these visions and dreams were precognitive and I would later hear about global or community events that I had seen in my visions days earlier.

It wasn't until I was in my late thirties that I knew I had more than a lucky guessing sense. I didn't feel confident talking to anyone about it because, for so long, I could not explain what I was experiencing.

It is not unusual for an empath or psychic intuitive to feel stifled as they carry so much energy from the unseen world within them, but are unable to fully understand it or put it to use. In a world that distrusts psychic sensing, many sensitives are socially conditioned to keep their gifts hidden.

I moved through life with fear of being left out, cast aside, or feeling the sting of societal judgements, misconceptions, and misunderstandings of revealing my true self. I felt alone, misunderstood, and judged and the consequences were devastating.

Lucky for me, my spiritual team has benevolently and without hesitation steered me to the path and teachers that have inspired me to own who I am.

My Awakening

My awakening had been stirring beneath the surface for my entire life, but really came to a head just after my second baby was born. I started to have very disturbing dreams that caused me much emotional turmoil, and these dreamtime experiences were so disturbing, that my waking reality was taken hostage and my ability to be an emotionally present mother was hanging by a thread. These dreams engulfed me and consumed me, and logical and introspective as I am, the details and mystery of their presence was sending me into an emotional insensibility. With two young children at home, who depended on me to be healthy and engaged, I went to see a counsellor recommended by my husband's *Employee Assistance Program*. After about a month of getting very little sleep, each night I would create mental games with myself so that I would not have to face the inevitability those dreams. I eventually forced myself to stay awake in the hopes that my exhaustion would somehow erase their presence, but to no avail. My only hope of a reprieve lay in getting in to see a counsellor as soon as possible. While I waited for my first appointment, which seemed like an eternity, I immersed myself into stacks of self-help books and audios.

I remember the day of my appointment distinctively. I literally ran into her humble home office and spewed every poured out all the pain, guilt, disgust, confusion, and negative feelings that filled me. I told her about my bizarre dreams, my exhaustion, and most importantly my desire to master this challenge without the use of medication. I felt exhausted, ashamed, disgusted, confused, and utterly frustrated, but I knew, at the deepest level of my being, I was not depressed.

Even so, I was experiencing a level of darkness that had be contemplating suicide on more than a few occasions. But every time self-doubt or self-loathing led me into a darkened pit, somehow a miraculous event or trigger would pull me back from the edge of utter despair. I look back now and I can see the profound celestial and angelic help in every dramatic life occurrence that unfolded that brought me to my knees in anguish and self-doubt. I sit here today typing these words because my team of guides intervened.

My counsellor provided a comforting and safe outlet for me to release the energy that had been blocking my ability to see the story that my guides were trying to share with me. She helped me to free myself from the darkness that held me captive every night. But most importantly, she prescribed some self-reflection and meditation techniques to try at home, for further healing and recovery.

I knew there was much inner work ahead for me, but at least I had someone to talk to and navigate these troubling emotions, which was the start to a new lifelong path of spiritual learning. I remember her telling me that whatever was surfacing was doing so because I was primed to deal with it. Our subconscious and our Higher Self never offers what we are not able to move beyond. This was profound for me, for I had encouragement and a sense that there was 'potential' for me to rise above it. When you feel the depths of darkness and despair that many experience, the notion of 'potential' is like a magical balm. I felt a profound healing and an energetic activation went off within me, and like a 'click' when everything flows in perfect timing, I instantly felt a Divine reason to rise above limitation and darkness.

The next morning, as the kids lay in bed sleeping and my husband was at work, I sat on the couch, put on some meditation music, and tried the breathing and visualization techniques she suggested. Within a few minutes, I felt a strange tingling sensation move throughout my body. I experienced a multi-dimensional spinning, spiralling, and turning, of which I can only explain as a Merkabah rotation. I was spinning in a multitude of directions all at once, and at a profound speed. I felt as though I was being lifted off the couch or as if I was levitating to match the frequency that was swirling within me. I began begging for answers, crying, and imbuing myself into the experience, as the exhaustion was allowing all of my logical defences to remain at bay so that I could experience what was meant to be experienced. I felt incredible love, light, and warmth seep into every cell, and as I was talking, I felt as if there was a being responding to my calls for help.

At the time, I didn't know who this being was, and it was only years later that I learned it was one of my magical spirit guides sent specifically to me for this profound healing experience. I called her my music guide, because of her powerfully healing abilities with colour and sound that brought me to state of transformation and awakening that very first day. She is a very powerful guide and not only will the experience be etched in my soul's memory for infinity, I often use this experience to amp-up my frequency if I am feeling low in my personal frequency.

I sat on my couch in this multi-dimensional experience, speaking to someone so beautiful and profound, who made me feel so unconditionally loved, supported, connected, and Divine. I sensed for the first time that I was far grander than I had ever imagined. Not only did I glimpse my potential, but also if this experience was possible, then I wondered, what else is there to experience.

In the swirling intoxication of her spirit essence, I wept and begged for answers. "Why me? Why must I experience this now?" And with every question, she would answer with a love, light, and calmness that was so profound, I still have difficulty describing it to this day. I can only say it was as close to an angelic and Godly experience as I have ever known to exist.

The meditation that day was my first initiation into the world of energy, spirit, and brilliance that can only be understood by those who have sunk to the depths and who have been lifted by the hand of spirit. For it is truly life altering, life changing, and beyond what earthly words can explain. The level of unconditional love allowed me the window of opportunity to know that I was more than I thought and believed, and this reality was much grander than I had ever experienced.

I came back to a waking conscious state as the spinning slowed and the voice disappeared. A light had diffused throughout my entire body. And though I returned soaked with my tears and perspiration as my body tried to process and regulate the intense healing that had occurred; I was forever changed. I still carry the memories of those treacherous dreams, but the light and vision of my heightened potential allowed me to move far beyond that devastated state. My life had new hope, with greater meaning, and I carried a new sense of belonging that I had never felt or even knew existed. I had begun the ancient and cosmic remembrance of who I would evolve into.

I knew there was much darkness to work through as I began the inner work that lay ahead, but at least I had such hope that potential I saw would bring light to a dark state of being. This loving angelic being allowed me to reconnect with spirit at a level to which I had never known even existed. In the following weeks, I moved forth in a state of renewal, and the synchronicity and energetic communication was delivered to me every day as I interacted with my guides.

For the first time in my somewhat lonely inner life, I felt like I was not alone. I knew I was guided, loved, protected, and supported beyond any earthly explanation and whatever I would ask for, be it help, guidance, or validation, a new energetic or synchronistic sign would be given. Besides the incredible birth of my children, this awakening was truly one of the most amazing experiences of my physical life.

After that magical day, I meditated every day and renewed

my commitment to a path of self-discovery. I began to learn and understand all I could about what it was that I had experienced that day. I was pulled into and onto several paths and all led me to a destination with answers to my questions.

Finally the veil had been lifted enough for me to see what I knew stirred within me since I was a child. I had always felt 'out of place,' 'different,' 'misunderstood,' and as a highly empathic and psychic kid, for the first time, the puzzle to my own personal soul story was beginning to unfold for me and I truly felt inspired to know more. Experiences, dreams, and impressions began to surface shortly after this healing meditation and like pieces to the energetic puzzle; my life's mysteries began to fall into place. Each new day brought new clues, cues, and symbols that would lead me on an unbelievable path.

I noticed a great increase in synchronicities, coincidences, and situations where my guides and I would play with communication and validation. The signs and symbols were always placed before me, as they had been throughout my entire life, only this time, I was awake, engaged, and passionate about this new turn of events.

Pleiadian Visitations

I have learned so many powerful lessons and gained insight beyond my imagining and all of it is unconditionally gifted from those that lovingly serve as they help us fulfil our soul plans. The Pleiadians are constant with their loving gifts of guidance and energetic work.

The Pleiadians really are humanity's seeded ancestors and their love and care for awakening is unparalleled. I am utterly grateful beyond earthly words for the honour, value, and love that I have discovered as I move through these profound experiences and learn the lessons shared by my celestial team to prepare me for open conscious contact.

I offer my utter gratitude to Wendy and the Pleiadians as well as the myriad of beings, who are with me on this profound journey, for your unconditional love and support.

My First Memory of a Pleiadian Visitation

My first Pleiadian experience occurred in 1975 when the world, in general, had little knowledge and concern about Universal energy and multi-dimensional aspects. In many of these experiences, however, due to the limiting belief systems, state of awareness, and the ability to safely

285

communicate in fear-based societies, these types of interactions would only bring harm or discomfort. So for now the visitations remain in higher consciousness states and slowly seep into our remembrance when we are ready to bring them to the surface for exploration.

The first physical visitation that I remember was when I was six years old. I was in our family home, sitting on the floor watching a popular program called *Hee Haw* with my family. I heard the doorbell ring and I got up to answer it. When I opened the door, I was pleasantly surprised to see the two characters, whom I'd just seen on the television, standing in front of me; two farmers with jean overalls and pitchforks. I felt honoured that these stars were at our door. "What a lucky day," I must have thought as I remembered the excitement of the experience.

This first visitation happened this way so that I would be triggered with this memory when the timing was appropriate for me to seek the answers to explain a number of odd experiences. These strange and unbelievable experiences are given so that we are triggered to seek within to understand them.

These are all manifestations of the Divine design to allow

your story to unfold. This memory was triggered as I began my ascension path a number of years ago and in perfect timing for me to seek the answers into its meaning. Other odd multi-dimensional experiences or memories would further my navigation on this amazing path of enlightenment and awakening, and they sometimes felt like a very surreal dream.

As we experience events like this, it is not uncommon to hesitate and ask, "Did this really happen, or was it a dream? It felt so real, so why does no one remember it but me?" I now know, we are given such experiences throughout our life and when we are ready, we will remember, thus triggering further expansion.

I remember walking out of my house to go with them, and at the age of six, I was placed in a state of energetic displacement, so that the experience could be completed. I was taken onto a ship with these beings whom I later learned were members of my Pleiadian family.

I now see higher realm beings in long light-coloured gowns when I am aboard their crafts, but at that time, they used cloaking and screen projections. This is common during initial contacts to enable humanity to get used to their presence and to endure that we are not sent into shock or distracted by their true forms. Higher frequency beings have the ability to create using only thought, so to manifest a new physical form is fluid and easy and done often in these experiences. I believe they used their intelligence and advanced technology to teleport me instantly and directly onto their ship. The purpose of that early visitation was to adjust my empathic energetic levels so that I would not go into a state psychic overload as I began to expand my social experiences in the greater world.

Six years old is when most children start school and being a highly empathic child, I would have felt everything from those around me. If left unaltered, my state of energetic absorption would have resulted in illness that would have most likely taken me away from the blueprint I had originally designed for myself.

My energetic abilities would have caused me a great deal of trouble if they had not been adjusted at that time. I can look back now and understand why I experienced the challenges that I had, as I did not understand how to filter the information I was sensing on a level that others didn't have or fathom. The odd experiences or memories, and dreams that always stood out, now make sense to me. The pieces of the puzzles that are forming my story has revealed itself to me as a brilliant plan.

As a result of this Pleiadian visitation, I was left with a three inch diameter red scar, directly above my heart that has been misdiagnosed many times by many dermatologists. I know now that this scar was to remind me of my place within the stars and the greater celestial family that is always watching, protecting, and guiding me and that my grander plan and potential should not be forgotten.

Celestial visitations from various members of my celestial family, and friends from other realms that have agreed to assist me on this journey, have occurred many times throughout my life. These visitation experiences were always timed for specific energetic shifts, or energetic manipulations to open me up, heal, or to activate certain pathways so that I have been able to sense more, retain data at an energetic level, and so on. Sometimes the visitations are merely amongst loved ones to remind me at the energetic level of why I am here and what I agreed to fulfil in this incarnation.

However challenging the density of this plane may be at times, it is one that I knew I could manoeuvre within, and my Higher Self, my spirit guides, and my celestial teams are lovingly committed to my journey. Help is usually required here in this transitional time, and at any stage we can ask for assistance, guidance, validation and help, and it will be given. I know that many times I have been drawn toward a path that would have taken me out of the game and each time my celestial team stepped in to redirect me and remind me of my greater plan.

This, and many other experiences, have given me the proof, the validation, and above all, the peace of mind of the greater existence that I am entangled with. I sense, I see, I feel a world that extends beyond what most people can see. This does not mean that I am any more special or different from others, for we all hold these experiences. I offer these stories so that those who may have felt or experienced similar energetic transformations will understand there is an overriding reason and timing for all of it. It truly is Divine.

These multi-dimensional occurrences drift into my life when I am ready to take my learning to a new level, and I always experience the underlying sensation of unconditional love and greater support as I unlock another piece to the puzzle that allows me to understand the Universe in a more expanded and loving way.

The energies of my grand story are delivered in story-like fragments, visions, or concepts and sometimes appear as a memory, a deja-vu, and sometimes as a vision within my meditation state, and of course often within my dreams. Many of the dreams that appear to have a surreal feeling or odd component are the result of the intuitive knowingness that is linked with actual visitations from members of our celestial teams.

My Pleiadian Bird Family

One of my most memorable multi-dimensional experiences is that of a journey to a Pleiadian ship one afternoon during a daily meditation. I began as I always do and I saw my energetic self-floating into the centre of a circular lightship. Immediately, I was brought into the presence of two tall beings dressed in long white robes. I later found out that these beings were members of my Pleiadian bird family and they were excited to be a part of my energetic alignment.

The bird people, who are primarily seventh dimensional vibrations, originated from the Lyran star system and migrated to the Pleiadian star system where thy joined the myriad of diverse beings that are assisting many of us on our ascension paths.

I remember standing in a circular lobby of the craft where we walked to a round table at which point they handed me a visor of some sort that I excitedly donned. I saw green symbols and patterns flowing downward in front of a black background. It was quite similar to a scene in the movie *The Matrix*, where we were shown the patterns of the matrix. I learned that the visor was an energetic tool, a decoder, used to alter my vision and allow me to see more of the energetic patterns that exists within our reality. I had aligned myself enough, at this point, to have some of these reality filters removed. We tend to dismiss the existence of these energetic elements of Creation that drift among us because we are not of the vibration and atunement to see what resides at the refined frequency state. Since that meditation, I have had many energetic adjustments that have altered my sensory and heart chakra areas and my sight to ultimately prepare me to receive conscious contact.

My visions, impressions, and memories continue to include a myriad of beings and experiences and become ever more energetically profound. I have found that the more I tune in to the process of ascension, engaging, and enmeshing with Gaia and the cosmos, the more I am gifted with energetic brilliance. There are aspects of our multi-dimensional existence that our physical mind simply cannot fathom, but the more open, loving, and accepting we are of ourselves, the grander and expansive the experiences will be. For multi-dimensional living is propelled from the heart and it is in the heart that we are all One.

I am learning about my greater family and my overall heritage within the greater existence and the platform that I create for others is one of respect and reverence for this energetic dance we are all entangled within. I have seen, experienced, and fallen back in love with myself in a deep way, the way that Creation loves us. When we awaken, we are imbued with the highest level of reverence for all that we now experience which is the highest vibration of unconditional love that we can find within for ourselves. Love is the most profound vibration in this Universe and it will open the door to every experience we desire.

Aligning and shifting from one vibrational frequency to another is possible and the techniques and concepts here are those that I have experienced with profound results. If I have been able to explore and experience other dimensional facets to our reality and existence then it is possible for anyone, and in this way, we all really share the same story as we seek the same glow of a new Earth.

A Celestial Light Show Celebration

In December 2014, I was treated to an amazing show of speed and light that gave me insight into concepts of time and space beyond our limited dimensional experience. Early one morning I gazed out to the star-filled sky and was telepathically engaged with Gaia and my celestial family. Usually when I am working with my lightships, there can be anywhere from three to about eight ships that make themselves known and link in with me. This particular day, as I gazed up the sky, there were at least thirty to forty lightships dancing and darting in the sky in grand celebration and my heart immediately filled with great love and excitement. This was a celebratory ceremony for me as I escalated and moved beyond a phase in my energetic work in preparation for contact.

I had been seeing these lightships hover in the sky above my home for a couple years, at this point, as they made their way closer to me, preparing my energy field and working with sight, auditory, and other sensory apparatus to allow me the greatest expansion in alignment with my ever-increasing passion and intent. That December morning, I was treated to a lightship celebration that was a cosmic sign that we had become entangled far beyond what I had originally anticipated and with more beings that I could have ever imagined.

The ships moved at speeds far beyond the constraints of human technology and the movements were so precise. I had wondered at their ability to dart and dance at such incredible speeds and not crash into one another. However, I learned that all the pilots were linked telepathically and because of their resonance, technology, and emotional and telepathic interfacing, they had the ability to collapse or expand time to suit their desires and needs. Their 6th to 8th dimensional perspectives gave them the ability to live within rules where time does not exist. This is also, why we can have visitations or meditation experiences that equate to several hours, yet only a few minutes pass.

That lovely morning, in celebration of the energetic demarcations that I had moved past, was truly special and a gift I will always treasure. This experience taught me that we have the potential to let go of our concept of time and space and slip into the speeds to which our frequency fits.

In these visitation experiences, whether in a physical form or within my dreams, I am discovering, as many others are too, that the ability to create can be as fluid as breathing if we are aligned. I now understand the bigger picture of why I am here and what my role is. All the dark experiences, where I felt alone and disconnected, have allowed me to empathize with those that wander in frustration, with a lack of direction and intimacy, as they are searching for something though they do not know what — yet.

The process of ascension and awakening has brought me profound peace and a sense of self-love that I have never felt before and it is all due to the allowance of following the intuitive guidance and synchronistic gifts from my multi-dimensional team. I no longer feel as if I am floundering or running. I have purpose, I have belonging, I have gained a level of confidence and honour for who I am within this grand plan. In my knowingness, my awakening, whatever I uncover and reveal to myself also affects the All. This Universal benevolence of a grander plan is what excites me to continue my seeking every day. I know now, as will you, to feel the guidance and surety in every step and know we are loved and honoured.

My Alchemical Evolution

My team offers assistance whenever I ask for it. Meditations and quiet reflection times are now used for the refinement of my thought processes and altering my energetic states, vision, and conditionings or patterns that hold me back from receiving what it is I desire at the highest levels. I have many experiences where my chakras and my cellular DNA structure literally feels as if it is spiralling, vibrating, and oscillating to keep up with the energy I am expanding into. As I work on refining my personal frequency, the symptoms vary and the multi-dimensional experiences feel more surreal every day.

The cells within my face vibrate, twitch, and jostle, as my core frequency and cells literally speed up with the potential to sense greater expansive realms and inter-dimensional frequencies. When I ask my team, "What are we doing?" I am told, "We are shifting you."

So I simply surrender into the experience and take it all in, and enjoy the energetic massage. The process of ascension is the slow and intermittent stretching of one's energetic body to fit the heightened and quickened states and it must be prepared for the upcoming shifts.

I can usually tell when we are about to move through something profound, energetically speaking. So as our planet is about to receive a new stream of pulsating celestial or solar fluctuations, I am usually already amped up before these shifts occur. We can be assured that timings of planetary pulsations usually occur at celestial and seasonal alignments, such as full moons, solstices, equinoxes, and so on. The benefits to this constant energetic balancing is profound. If I go into a meditation with an ailment, concern, or issue that I need to move through, or even if I am just feeling over-tired, I can come out of my meditation completely rebalanced, harmonic, and peaceful. I feel as if I have had a three-hour nap but in actuality, my meditation is only about eighteen minutes.

Dematerializing

One day, a few years ago, I began my meditation as I always do with deep breathing, a white light prayer, and a grounding visualization with Gaia. I quickly began to feel my state of consciousness transform.

In this meditative experience, I saw my energetic self, the higher aspect of who I was, fly up into the etheric space of our galaxy. In the excitement of what I experienced, I did not see the profound being that was floating with me and in front of me — at least at first. Eventually he caught my attention when I heard him talking to me about what was happening to Earth and the changes that humanity is experiencing is the result of these greater planetary adjustments.

I was enamoured with the beauty of Earth as he guided me further up into the ethers. The being looked like what I imagined Jesus or John the Baptist looked like. It could very well have been one of my spirit guides cloaked in the image of what I understood to be this being's profound energy, so that I would pay close attention. He appeared in front of me and he was dressed in a camel-cloth robe tied at the waist and he projected a gentle, yet profound sense of surety, that impelled me follow and listen intently.

As I continued to float, He directed my attention with his arms and explained to me what was what was happening to Gaia, and what my role was in the greater plan, I felt the giddiness of a new apprentice to a great master who honoured me by bestowing His wisdom directly to me.

I missed some of what he taught me as I was a bit overwhelmed by the profound experience particularly when my body shifted into an altered state. I realized then that I was fully aware and essentially in charge of this unusual experience. I began to see my energetic body dematerialize and split off in an infinite number of pieces and directions as they sped into deep space to inter-mingle with the collective vibrations. The particles, that make up who I am, seemed to disintegrate, dematerialize, and disperse into the cosmos, yet I was conscious about their presence. I immediately transcended into pure spirit essence, conscious within the heightened state to see myself both as a singular individual and as a dematerialized being that was infused into All That Is.

The profundity of what I was experiencing allowed me to understand at the conscious level that within heightened state of a 5th dimensional frequency, we can choose how we desire to experience that frequency. The 5th dimensional potential, and the skills and ability that we have command over, can support our desire to create the ability to be in one physical place and experience a singular reality plane, or we can choose to dematerialize and break off to gain the collective perspective of the same experience.

I was so excited and amazed at this experience that I withdrew my attention from the teacher before me. We were so high above Earth that it appeared to be the size of a large pumpkin. Gaia's gorgeous blue and green hues felt so inspiring, and for a split second, I felt the profound love for Gaia that keeps many of us coming back lifetime after lifetime. My guide allowed me this profound experience and I know that as I grow and expand, I will enjoy more experiences like this.

My Multi-Dimensional Self

I came to this role of Universal Unity as an ambassador of new Earth as part of the natural process of my own integration and expansion. Just as all of you lay the groundwork for what you came here to pursue, so too was I offered this task as a directional guide as I make my way on my own path of ascension. For in other realms and in other star systems, I have assisted planets in reconciliation and peacemaking strategies in warring times and conflict. Many souls take on roles that are similar to the roles we play in other vibrational frequencies to allow for the continuity of expansion in any one direction. Other souls take on very different roles in every lifetime so our blueprints can really challenge us.

Even if we do not consciously remember it, our Higher Self is always patiently guiding us to a perfectly aligned path with our soul's desire to evolve. These wonderful inter-stellar meetings, reunions, and planning committees are so very gratifying and as we awaken and merge with our celestial family, we will begin to remember the roles in which we have all played together in this Universal family.

In first landings and first contact experiences, we will be met with those of our direct family and those beings that are of our closest physical ancestors. We will be eased into the diversity that exists within our multi-dimensional Universe and this is the profound thread-work of Creation. Higher states of consciousness bring us closer in connection, as a collective, with Gaia, and allow us the potential to reunite in spirit essence in the common love and light to serve the Divine Plan.

These energetic, higher consciousness experiences will become more evident in our mainstream discussions, and eventually the entertainment media will express their opinions and perceptions about these shifts as well. Our multi-dimensional experiences are a natural part of our genetic encoding and this process is allowing us to play a bigger part in this cosmic story of Gaia's ascension. My dear lighted ones, in all of the challenges we may face, know that these experiences are designed solely by us, for us. We all knew our potential for ascension would be a possibility within *this* lifetime and at some level, we all wanted to play a part within it. We have perfectly timed these situations and celestial unfolding because we knew we had the power to merge with it. Honor and embrace who you are morphing into as it means you are listening and acting upon your highest and best path.

Gaia's ascension will prompt the awakening of many beings and in this awakening; we are moved to partake in whatever level we can integrate within. Ascension allows us to fully embrace all that we are in every moment. As we expand and rediscover a new aspect of our infinite potential, we move on to seek a deeper level of understanding to our profound Universe and our Oneness within it. Embrace all that you are for you are a precious, brilliant, glorious aspect of Creation and you are just as multi-dimensional as the angelic realms that serve you. For we are all One!

The myriad of multi-dimensional realms and beings that I encounter on my path is a great honour and I always offer reverence during these experiences. This work requires a high level of respect as we ascend into higher levels of awareness. Each day offers new experiences, lessons, and a myriad of new paths. I am committed to remaining a steady daily practice of reflection so that I may continue to move with these ever changing and accelerating times. As I am learning to manoeuvre and navigate my way around, deciphering the refined energetic stories and symbols, I understand that there are always lessons within each experience. I am seeing the link of what I am doing, here on this planet, and the role that I have created for myself, within my blueprint, as one that I also play in other realms and councils.

Chapter XIV

Conclusion

What if all species lived in harmony and we had the ability to survive in our healthiest states without disease and illness and all animals could live in peace within a symbiotic world? What if our oceans and soils were brought back to pure health and were able to sustain new species and life forms? What if we have the potential to experience life without a monetary system? What if we were able to live toxin free, pollution free, and with the highest regard for all species and potential for one another? What if all debt was forgiven and all desires were manifested instantly merely by thought? What if we could travel through the star systems instantly and safely merely by thought projection and mastery of personal resonance and Universal laws of energy? What if we were to have unlimited access to Universal knowledge and we had the ability to experience all life at all levels of spirit? Allow the what if to surprise you in what you truly know and what you truly desire for if we never ask the questions, we never know the profundity to which we can create new potentials for humanity and our cosmos.

Ascension is the process of remembrance into the Divine aspect as we move from the individual *I AM* state of being, and extend our consciousness to the *I AM THAT I AM* state of consciousness. Ascension allows us to remember how we operate on higher levels and understand that we are enmeshed and linked with All That Is, Source, and life at every level.

As ascending beings, we no longer have to experience struggle, or poverty, or lack, for if we understand what we can create, then we are on the path to new Earth. The façade of the old world human, through inner self reflection and profound self-discovery, will gracefully step up into the resting place of a glowing, illuminated 5th dimensional new Earth as it was designed to be. As Gaia soaks in the glow of a new dawn, we will experience our infinite potential in all ways, because we know that all we have ever desired has always been within, and this, dear lighted ones, is truly profound.

Acknowledging your profundity is at the core of all ascension work, for it ignites our direct link to Source and all within Creation. Your true natural spirit essence illuminates and sparkles all that you touch, when these entanglements are remembered and thus, you leave your energetic imprint upon Creation.

Profundity is not the human-self over-flowing with ego, it is in the deep seeded reverence for the Divine and that we walk in knowingness. It is also, what masters knew within every cell of their vessels, that every life is valued and every life is Divine. The essence and Divine spark that resides within you is your link. The association and entanglement that we have with Source will inspire and ignite us to enable the veil of illusions, borders, separation, and limitation to disappear; healed by the cosmic pulse of unconditional love.

As our ascension is unfolding, we align our greater energetic selves to the level where contact with higher realm beings is possible. The more we open our knowingness to the infinite and the expansiveness of who we are as multi-dimensional spirit essence, it sends out beams of vibrations at the speed of light to others in the Universe to connect with us. This is how Universal energy works, and we are a part of it! This is a fact.

Contact is the essence of connection. Contact is the

integration of all that we've learned and expanded into, to the point where we allow for the opportunity to be reunited with our greater galactic families. As each of us awakens, the energy streams of contact increase in strength and power, and we bring ourselves to the point where landing parties are not only a scene from a Hollywood movie, but a reality to benefit the All. The vibration resonance of unconditional love will allow us to eventually step up to the level of guide and teacher to other newly awakening planets. We may, one day return the energetic gift that is being gifted to us now.

As we merge into the sea of stars, we become greater and grander than we were before. This is our story, our play, and our song. We surrender into what's occurring and we're excited about what we're creating, and it can be seen in the healing and expansive wave that now touches every corner of our ascending world. Be not afraid of change, and be not afraid of what resides within, for you have the power to overcome and see it through, because you were the master creator in it all. It's time to embrace who you are, for we are all the pulse within Creation.

The cosmos awakens in delight and celebration, and in the

myriad of incarnations, we meet in this resting place where our souls can breathe again. Beings from thousands of star systems and planets rise in jubilation as we burn brightly in our new 5th dimensional skin, and the glow is bouncing off every being within Creation. The path was truly profound, and here we all stand, in various frequencies and forms, as we enter into a new energetic agreement and paradigm, for humanity and New Earth.

This is just a small sample of what's possible if we expand our mindset to dream and explore the infinite possibilities that have always resided within. Our celestial family is standing by and they are more than ready to align us for first contact and other advanced teachings of ascended planets. All that we can be excitedly drawn to is on the horizon for us to discover in the Universal expanse of infinite potential.

Know that if you feel stuck, or depressed and confused, that you own the power and ability to feel profound. Know that you are profound and infinite with every fiber of your being and your reality will show you this frequency with what you manifest, and with the synchronicity that unfolds.

So go forth and create your path with all the brilliance that you chose to colour your experience. This light you carry is grand and bold and it is only you that can carry it. We are each unique and we are also the same. It is in this sameness and this uniqueness that we see one another in each other's eyes and in this, we build the bridge to a New Earth, as the cosmos rejoices in celebration.

~ Namaste ~

Practical Tips

Prepare for Ascension and Higher Dimensional Living

The desire to know and answer the call of your soul's blueprint means that you honour yourself enough to want to uncover the potential you know resides within you. Ascension is about the unveiling of your natural spirit essence and gaining a greater perspective for your potential, our planets potential, and the benevolent Universe that we are all entangled with.

There is much to do to prepare for the inevitable first landings. We need to ensure we are personally within a balanced state of love and acceptance of ourselves and one another, here on Earth, by creating intelligent dialogue in our communities and social systems. There are many issues for us to work through at home, before we can honestly say we are ready to honour and embrace those of another realm and galactic community and council. The variance in energy states is a very real thing and until we are able to fully release the fears, judgements, and aggressions that block our potential, we cannot readily offer a landing pad to our celestial family.

311

- Conduct inner reflective work to understand, and then release all judgements, fears, and biases in order to gain a neutral and compassionate state. *What do I believe to be true about who I am and what I exist within?*

- Express excitement and joy in your efforts to prepare yourself and the world for improved international relationships within our world. The joy will promote healing for Gaia and the improved international relationships will prepare us for extended world and planetary/cosmic contact.

- Acknowledge your profundity within Creation and embrace all that you are! Living authentically puts you in the vibration of self-love, self-honour, and ecstasy.

- Integrate new ways of 'being' by getting clear on what beliefs, definitions, and conditionings we have. This allows you to tap into the hidden aspects of who you are, expanding upon what you believe in positive, loving, and creative ways.

- Practice your innate abilities and communication skills with your energetic team through the processes of heightened consciousness states. Dreams, meditations, and expanded states of consciousness bring you in alignment with your true self and with beings of higher resonance.

- Create positive and integrative dialogue with our youth and children for they are the light bearers of a new generation to lead our planet on new paths of peace, love, acceptance, and harmony.

- Create thought-expanding dialogue about unity and oneness with all beings. The ideas and visions we have for a peaceful, healthy, and non-toxic Earth are the road map toward our destiny.

- Allow the unique light of all beings to shine as it was created to do. All paths are equally important, valid, and valued.

- Declare your intent and create your path with profound knowingness that you are a powerful creator. As you KNOW, as you INTEND, as you RELEASE, as you ALIGN, as you TRUST, and as you ALLOW you set the stage and pace for enlightenment, ascension, and contact with our celestial family. The more you know about yourself, the clearer your path will be.

Recommended Reading

Books have always been my window into understanding our infinite potential. Like peeking into the unknown, books allow us the opportunity to alter and shift our core frequency by expanding our awareness into heightened potentials of new ideas and concepts. Reading offers the possibility of integration and expansion and allows us to taste the hidden realms of our potential. It is important to explore every book and every social platform that resonates with you. Follow your excitement and trust your intuition, because you never know what path the next page or the next chapter may introduce to you. Adventures and greater alignment await for those brave enough to explore the unknown.

Re-reading books can offer new insights into not only the original message, but also to push you to new heightened states that you were not prepared for at first reading. Along the path of your ascension, and with every new thought, you will literally change the landscape of the path you create for yourself. Every aspect of who you are is altered as you offer new concepts and ideas that were previously unknown. Thus, reading powerful books over, especially ones that deeply resonate with you, is a wonderful way to not only continue your learning and expansion, but to cement the infinite possibility of what you are able to create with these expanded notions.

All of these books have been instrumental in my spiritual growth and guides on my path of ascension. I have the deepest of gratitude to the authors, the teachers, and the light-workers for their integrity and passion for this work. Your light and wisdom is a gift to humankind.

Songs of the Arcturians: Arcturian Star Chronicles, Volume I, by Patricia Pereira

Eagles of the New Dawn: Arcturian Star Chronicles, Volume II, by Patricia Pereira

Songs of Malantor: Arcturian Star Chronicles, Volume III, by Patrica Pereira

Arcturian Songs of the Masters of Light: Arcturian Star

Chronicles, Volume IV, by Patricia Pereira

For a lengthier listing of soul expanding books, please refer to this link: http://universalunity.ca/books/

About the Author

Joanna L. Ross was born and raised in Victoria, British Columbia. She relocated to Vancouver in her twenties where she worked for a number of years at various public and private sector jobs. Joanna was always drawn to the mysteries and wonders of life and her conscious shift to metaphysics came after the birth of her second child when she was beset with a series of soul-wrenching dreams. After being prescribed meditation as a way to make peace with these dreams, she found herself firmly planted on a path that made her innate psychic abilities self-evident. She found herself exploring and entangling with the world of energy that is outside of physical perception.

At this time, Joanna found herself in a higher sate of consciousness and she met her spirit guides -- multi-dimensional and energetic beings of a myriad of forms and species. Over the years, these cosmic friends and family began to introduce themselves and she is blessed by their presence in all aspects of her daily life and worldly travels. Joanna answered the call to explore and disseminate the potentials and offerings of this vast cosmos as she experiences the sometimes unfathomable process of ascension.

Joanna's first remembrance of contact with her celestial family was at the age of five and this left a lasting and very loving impression upon her. Later the memory of the experience resurfaced and her true awakening began and the ensuing profound synchronistic events inspired an intense desire to understand the multi-dimensional realms she experienced during these early meditations. Now she is devoted to exploring the path and the offerings of our infinite Universe.

Joanna now lives a harmonious life in Calgary, Alberta with her family. She loves creating artwork, and guiding her children and other families to experience the joy and fulfilment achieved when they connect to our Universe and their expanded potential. Joanna's primary passion and life goal is to study and serve Creation. In utter gratitude, she is inspired to share, educate, and enlighten those who desire to understand ascension, Universal Laws, and our greater Universal family within the cosmos.

Joanna now lives a harmonious life in Calgary, Alberta with her family. She is inspired to share, educate, and enlighten those who desire to understand ascension, Universal Laws, and the greater Universal family that humanity is now awakening. Joanna enjoys teaching about the elegance of preparing for expansive entanglement with our multi-dimensional family, the world beyond Earth's atmospheric borders and the stirring of Source within all life.

Joanna, the founder of Universal Unity, is an intuitive visionary, public speaker, esoteric wisdom instructor, author, and Ambassador for Universal Unity. Joanna offers the Universal Unity platform as a portal to all things that relate to our insatiable curiosity to heighten our awareness, grow in love and light as we create the frequency for a new 5th Dimensional Earth.

"In the process of ascension, we not only gain a greater understanding of the Universe and our role within it, we also gain insight into our expansive multi-dimensional celestial families and the spiritual path we walk as a collective upon Gaia."

Made in the USA
Coppell, TX
11 January 2020

14336986R20193